The Enoch Lifestyle

The Enoch Lifestyle

Faith vs. Fear

Albert Amara

Hunter Heart Publishing
DuPont, Washington 98327

The Enoch Lifestyle

Hunter Heart Publishing, LLC
DuPont, Washington 98327
www.hunterheartpublishing.com

Cover designer: Exousia Marketing Group, LLC
www.exousiamg.com

ISBN 13: 978-0-9823944-2-7

Printed in the United States of America.

<u>Dedication</u>

I dedicate this work to all those who have lost a loved one, either physically or otherwise to the fight against the terrors of every-day life, whether it be through gang violence, terrorist activity (9/11/2001 and all else), or through the financial crisis which has taken the world by surprise. These are trying days, and fathers are walking out on families, because of financial droughts, but on the other hand there are others who are so scared to travel or go to work, because of the fear of what will happen; that they are held prisoner in their own homes. If you are in these situations, please hold fast to the Word of God. Your help will soon appear.

~Albert Amara

Acknowledgments

It is with deep gratitude and appreciation that I express my sincere thanks to the following who have contributed in one way or the other to the accomplishment of this work:

- ➤ To the Lord and master of my life Jesus Christ, who gave me the gift to write, and also the inspiration for "The Enoch Lifestyle." There are many writers in the world, but He chose me to write this best seller, and I am extremely grateful for that.

- ➤ To my best friend and love of my life (my wife) Hilary, who encourages me to keep on writing.

- ➤ To my pastors and mentors Drs. W.J. and Kristie Moreland, whom I have watched and followed for over four years; learning from them the things that pertain to the Kingdom and life as it comes across the pulpit, and also in their nonverbal communications, which sometimes speak more volumes than words.

- ➤ To the editor and publisher of "The Enoch Lifestyle" Deborah Hunter, who was more than patient with me in the completion of this work. I had to pull this book many times to add fresh inspiration that I received from the Lord, but since this was a ministry to her first before a business, there were no complaints from her (Ma'am, I love you and your family, and it is only the good Lord who will reward you and your family for your love and patience. I thank God that I indeed made the right decision to place this best seller in your hands.)

Foreword

I was most honored to be asked to write this foreword for a true Son in the Faith. I have watched Albert grow over the years as a member, minister, and now, as a mentor, through his proficient writing style.

In his book, Albert does a wonderful and skillful job in laying out a blue-print for successful living. In the "Enoch Lifestyle", we learn how to develop a true relationship with our Heavenly Father, leading us to a fulfilled life. With insight, which comes from years of living in Sierra Leone, West Africa, and a grounded relationship with God our Father, he is able to lay out this powerful book.

If the Body of Christ is going to reach its full potential in the 21st Century, it is vital to understand the "Enoch Lifestyle." I recommend this book for all Believers who are ready to move into the fullness of the Kingdom of God, and walk in a dimension that the world is waiting to see.

The "Enoch Lifestyle" creates a sincere hunger for the Kingdom of God; to grow up and become a Son, and not just a child of God. The old Army motto, "Be all you can be", is a clarion call to the Body of Christ.

Read this book several times to transform your life into the predestined life God planned for you before the foundation of the world. I pray that you not only enjoy this book, and I know you will; but more importantly, let the pages transform you.

Dr. Will Moreland
Senior Pastor
International Gospel Church
Kitzingen, Germany

"It is risky not to take risks."
-Archbishop Benson Idahosa

Table of Contents

CHAPTER 1

WHY THE ENOCH LIFESTYLE?

THE SITUATION AT HAND

Imagine you are in West Africa, in the diamond rich country called Sierra Leone. The country has been in civil war for about a decade, but the government has assured you that everything is under control, and that there is no reason for fear. They had promised that the fighting is only in the rural parts of the country, and that it will never reach the capital city where you live. Also, to augment your faith in the system, there is a heavy presence of armed military personnel in the city, standing guard on almost every street corner. The presence of other West African forces still in the city parading the streets with heavy artillery, gives an added sense of security. Therefore, you abandon the plans you had to flee the country to seek refuge in another land. Your government has promised you, and so you take that promise to the bank, believing in it with all your heart.

Then all of a sudden, one clear evening, disaster strikes. You are sitting outside enjoying the cool of the evening, the twinkling stars shining ever so bright on that eve, when you hear gunshots. The sound is really not a strange sound, as the military fire shots all the time when driving around to warn of their presence, so you ignore it. Then, you hear it again, but this time it is even louder and there is not one, but dozens of rifle fire. Then, word spreads that the rebels (insurgents) have captured the city, and that they are fast approaching the heart of the city to take control of key targets there. At that moment, the thing that strikes you is, "What a fool I've been. Why didn't I leave when I had the opportunity?" You have heard of how these rebels enter a city, and how fear envelops the whole town.

The normalcy of life stops existing, as these thoughts go through your mind: *they recruit little boys sometimes as young as seven, to become freedom fighters.* To initiate these boys, they will give them rifles (AK-47) to kill all that resist their reign of terror, including the family members of the young recruits, just like gangs do in western countries to overcome the fear of killing someone. The young children who refuse to follow these hard initiation processes are considered not fit for battle, and therefore added to the number for execution. Brothers are forced to have sex with their sisters and fathers with their daughters. Sometimes, for no reason, they will enter a city and ask people to choose between short sleeves and long sleeves, as they are about to chop off their arms. If the people choose long sleeves, then their arms will be chopped off at the wrists, and if they choose short sleeves, they will be chopped off at the elbow.

At times, when they are just bored (basically people have not irritated them, but they still want to live up to their nature of evil), and a pregnant woman passes by, they will argue over the sex of the fetus and if they don't agree on the sex, they will cut the baby out with no anesthesia, and leave mother and child to die. If they feel like people are disgruntled towards them, they will tell that entire region, or the people present, to sing for them songs of praise. If they have the slightest inclination that someone is sad, it is death, or if they are not in the mood for shedding blood, then it is public flogging. All of these thoughts are going through your mind all at once, but you can't help but wonder what the pain will be like when your arm is chopped off. You have a situation at hand, but your main question is, "What do I do now?"

THE SPIRIT OF FEAR

That question is the purpose of this book, "The Enoch Life-style." You might not be in Sierra Leone, or any other place where there is a guerilla war, but if you are facing your own giant, in the form of fear of any type, please don't drop this book. Read on, and the Holy Spirit will interpret it to your spirit. For some of you who read the narrative above, you don't have to imagine far, because you were there in the heat of the sun, being chased by vigilant men pelting AK-47 rounds down your path, as you ran for your life. You were so shaken up by fear that you'd rather starve in your house in some undisclosed hide out than step out in the city to look for food. You had to learn the secret of cover and concealment – what the US Army spends well over $20,000 to train me (I am presently in the US Army), and many others to survive in a war that we may never get to fight in. However, for you it was not optional, as you had to learn and execute at the spur of the moment. Sometimes that means covering your baby's mouth until he/she is literally lifeless, because if you were discovered, you and the baby were left at the mercy of the merciless warlords.

Fear is crippling, and will cause a well-armed soldier to lose a fight to one who brought only a pocketknife to the battle. Satan, our enemy, hates the human race and his goal is to rule over us with total dominance, so that we can live in total fear. Just as those people in Sierra Leone, West Africa (where I was born) were in a state of total surrender under the rebel forces, so he wants his demons to control the whole world. He has been trying all throughout history to do that; using mankind to dominate his own kind. That was what happened in the World Wars and every major combat that has been fought, including the attack of America on 9/11 of 2001.

The devil wants you to be so paralyzed by fear that you cannot fly by plane for fear of terrorists, or that you cannot go to some neighborhood to evangelize for fear of gang violence, or do anything productive. What we have to realize is that fear is really a thief, and if you pay attention to it; it surely will rob you of your purpose. That was what happened after the attack on America on 9/11 that caused the airline industry to almost crumble in loss of business, because people were afraid of flying. In our cities today, the fear of guns and gun violence used by gangs and other groups sends its own chill down the spine of inhabitants of metropolitan cities, and it is like we are trapped in our own homes. How long can we afford to live like that? It is high time we realize that even though the devil rules by fear, the Lamb that sits on the throne, who is worthy of the praise, has shed His blood for us – Jesus Christ. He descended to hell and made the devil captive, putting him under our feet; therefore, we don't have to be afraid of him any longer. Because of Him, we do not have to live in fear, but in total faith. The great thing about this is that there is an answer for every fear in the Word of God, and that is what I will be using to expose the enemy in this book.

Friend, have you ever imagined what your life will be like if you get rid of all your fears? All of our sleepless nights, anxiety, and lack of peace can be traced in one way or the other to fear. Worry, doubt, unbelief, or whatever you can call it can all be traced to some-how or somewhere us taking our eyes off of our God. We somehow have managed to pick up our burdens again and carry them, instead of casting them on the Lord. This example of the faith of Enoch is for us saints in this 21st century to use to overcome everyday 21st century challenges that come to challenge our faith through fear. Fear is indeed the ultimate enemy of faith, and with it being present in any situation, we cannot have the victory. Every fear is learned. That is why if you let it, a baby can play with a venomous snake and think that it is a toy. That baby has not learned to fear yet, but as soon as it is taught that it is supposed to be afraid of that reptile, the fear is born and will stay with it for life. (I am not suggesting that you give your baby a viper as a pet).

Children and babies are the perfect example of how we are supposed to act in regards to fear. They have total trust in their parents that they will take care of them. I believe that is why the Lord loves them so much, and uses them often in scripture. The popular experiment of the baby and the puppy is an example of how we reinforce the fear in a baby. The baby is put in a crib with a puppy, and the mother is at a distance watching. The baby starts to cry and the mother, not wanting her baby to be afraid of the puppy, runs and picks up her baby to get it out of harms way. She really does not know what she has done, because by picking up the baby, the fear of the puppy is automatically reinforced, and that baby may be afraid of dogs for life. Whereas, if she had picked up the puppy, that would have let the baby think, "Oh, mummy is playing with the dog, it must be harmless then." Then, the chances of that child being afraid of dogs in the future will greatly reduce.

This is how the Lord wants us to treat fear; whether it comes in the form of gang activities in your neighborhood, terrorists, or financial situations. God wants us to rest in Him like Jesus rested in the boat when He and His disciples were crossing the sea of Galilee, and the waves were beating into the boat, almost causing it to sink (Mark 4:35 - 42). If we can only look at fear in the face and scoff at it saying, "I am not moved," we will have the Lord's attention faster than when we panic and run the way of the ones who don't know the God of Abraham. That is when God will start boasting about us, and our faith will increase. Faith is really like a muscle. The more you exercise it; the more it grows. Jesus Christ, our perfect example, demonstrated that for us in the scriptures. In His ministry of raising the dead, He went from raising Jairus' daughter, having to get everyone out of the room, to the raising of the widow's son, who was on the way to the cemetery, to Lazarus, who was dead for over four days and whom He had to call from the dead, without even touching him. I don't know why the Holy Spirit decided to put the sequence of those events together in that order, but what I learned from this is that the Lord Himself had to go from faith to faith. Maybe it was for our learning, because the scriptures state that He, the Lord, had the Spirit without measure.

DEFINITION OF ENOCH

There are a couple of verses of scripture that have puzzled theologians and scholars of the Bible over the years, and if ignored, can leave a big vacuum in the image, nature, and the likeness of our God. Those scriptures are in Genesis chapter 5 verses 21 –24:

21 "Enoch lived sixty-five years, and begot Methuselah. 22 After he begot Methuselah, Enoch walked with God three hundred years, and had sons and daughters. 23 So all the days of Enoch were three hundred and sixty-five years. 24 And Enoch walked with God; and he was not, for God took him."

The part that intrigues many scholars is the last verse, which states that Enoch was not found, because God took him (he did not die). However, between verse 21, when he had Methuselah, and thereafter made up his mind to follow God with all his might, and verse 24, when God took him, a whole lot of "living" transpired, and that is what we forget about. I want to bring out that "living" in 21st century language.

When we think of the man Enoch, we sometimes think that he was a superhuman person who was destined to be taken to heaven, regardless of however he lived his life. The other extreme is that Enoch lived like a hermit in total seclusion, so that he could not sin. But this is not so, as the above scripture let's us see. He was born into sin just like every man that came after Adam, and was the seventh from Adam. However, something happened to the man after he had his son Methuselah. He had an epiphany of the deity of the One and true God, amidst the wickedness and iniquity of his day, and he resolute in his mind to follow this God all the way.

Enoch must have heard stories of the peaceful presence of this great God from his great granddaddy Adam, who was still living when Enoch was a young man, being that people in those days lived to be almost a thousand years old. He heard about the authority and dominion that Adam had, and about how he was the one who named every beast of the field and every bird of the air (Genesis 2:19), even the ones that they were afraid of. I believe what intrigued this young man above all were the stories of the visits made by this God in the Garden of Eden, the sweet fellowship between Him and Adam, and the lack of the knowledge of time. O, how he longed to be the in the presence of this God; how he wanted to be pleasing to Him. Therefore, at the tender age of sixty-five (that was really young at that time), he made up his mind to go all the way in God, and that he did for three-hundred years when one day, God took him up from the earth.

This was the first man after Adam who walked with God so closely, as if it were in the Garden of Eden before sin entered the world. In those days, there was no restraint on the actions of men, and it was to the point that God said in Genesis 6:3 that His Spirit will not strive with man, so He cut down the age limit from about a thousand to one hundred and twenty years. But Enoch's walk with God was so intense that it gave the Almighty God memories of how He used to walk with His son Adam in the Garden. Therefore, God rewarded him by not allowing his physical body to be eaten up by death. He was taken up into heaven where he will be until the Lord comes with that triumphant army to take over the governing of the world.

THE FAITH OF ENOCH

The scriptures state in Hebrews 11:5: *"By faith Enoch was taken away so that he did not see death, **and was not found, because God had taken him**; for before he was taken he had this testimony, that he pleased God."* It is impossible to affect your generation the way Enoch did by living in seclusion from it. He demonstrated some-thing a lot of believers in this 21st century find challenging to do; that is to live a life pleasing to God. That life that is pleasing to God is one of faith. When you hear people talking about Enoch, you will hear a lot of how he lived a holy life, not defiling himself with the filth of his generation, and about how he did not sin like other men. While that is true, nothing much is being said about how he defeated the challenges of his time through his faith in God. If you are not careful, you will think this holy man of God lived in seclusion from his generation, even putting his experience with God on a pedestal, thinking that he was one of those who were destined to live that way and also, that we can never attain that level in God again. But that is completely false, as the name "Enoch" gives us clues as to how he got to that level. Enoch is a Hebrew name of a male child, which simply means *devoted* or *dedicated*.

The man made a conscious and deliberate decision of devoting his life to God, and he did it by living a life of faith. Why did the scriptures tell us in verse 5 of Hebrews 11 that it was by faith that Enoch was taken away? Why didn't it say that it was by holiness that he did not taste of death? It is because faith is what will move a person to the place of holiness and not the other way around. Without faith it is impossible to please God (Heb. 11:6). One thing I have found out in the scriptures and in this walk with God is that it is impossible to be a holy man of God without being a man of faith. Hebrews 11:6 (the famous verse in the Bible that talks about how we can please God), is preceded by the mention of the life of Enoch in verse 5, which is a build-up to verse 6. That was another way God was honoring Enoch in His all time best selling book (the Bible), because of how much of an impact he made on his generation through a life of faith.

In the Kingdom of God there is nothing greater than love. The Bible tells us that God Himself is love, and also our faith works through love. However, if you are going to have victory in Christ, you will need faith in God. Nothing gets done in God without faith. You believed in Jesus Christ and accepted Him into your life (if you have done so), without even physically seeing Him. That is faith. Even to live a holy life, you need faith in a God whom you have not seen to abstain from the works of the flesh. You have to believe that He sees that you are not giving in to that temptation, and He that saw in secret will reward you openly. As a matter of fact, sin is not only committing wicked acts of iniquity, such as adultery, murder, and the so called major sins that we are ashamed of talking about, but as Romans 14:23 states, *anything not done in faith is indeed sin.*

Faith is indeed connected to everything we do in God. That is what Enoch had that set him apart from everyone in his own time. There is no excuse for us not to do more than what Enoch did, as we are now under a better covenant (Heb. 8:6). A lot of people would say, "I would have been more committed to God, if I didn't have these kids or a spouse that I have to attend to." In Gen. 5:22, we see that Enoch was a family man; he had a wife and sons and daughters, but that did not stop him from pleasing God. That is the excuse of a lot of believers today – family, but the God who gave us our families is truly able to give us the grace to serve Him with those families if we do trust Him.

Enoch conquered every fear that was to be conquered, and that is why he had the victory. He literally received the victory through his faith in God. His relationship with his God was so intense that he started to walk like God here on earth. He had total dominion and was not afraid of a single fear that challenged his faith. Someone may ask why I am so confident that it was fear that Enoch overcame that made him please God to the point that God had to take him out of this world. To that I will say this: FEAR, which is False Evidences Appearing Real, is the complete opposite of faith, and if God in Hebrews 11:5 tells us that the patriarch Enoch had this testimony that he pleased Him (God), then we better believe it. The next verse of that scripture also tells us that without faith it is impossible to please God. This mighty man of faith lived in a time when men were starting to increase on the face of the earth, and their ways were evil. Therefore, God, seeing that Enoch had no more battles to win, took him up to heaven. I am not suggesting that if you live like this Patriarch lived you will be taken to heaven without dying, before death. What good will we be in heaven to God, while the earth perishes? One thing is certain; if you follow this life of faith, you will please God.

THE BULLS-EYE OF GOD'S WILL

Imagine you are playing the game of darts. You have a circular board and it is divided into circular segments that get smaller as you get to the center. You have so many chances to hit the center of the board, which is the bulls-eye. Every time you hit the bulls-eye, you score the most points at that particular time of the game. However, if you hit lesser than that, there is a possibility that someone will get a greater score than you, which will eventually make you finish the game longer than expected, and also finish in second or last place. In reality, the will of God and faith works like that. God has mapped out a plan for your life, and though you might not imagine some of the things that God has planned for you, it still does not mean that God has willed those things for you. Think of the will of God as that dartboard, and your faith is the dart that is used to hit the target. Even though you might hit outside of the bulls-eye at every strike, God is intending for you, and (even me), to hit the Bulls-eye every time you have an opportunity to strike, so that you can get to your purpose faster.

That is His will for us, and we have to realize that. That is why He is telling us that anything not done in faith is sin. Faith is that vehicle that will get you to your purpose, because as I said earlier, there are some things God will tell you through prophecy to accomplish that you will literally say to yourself, " Oh not me. He must have the wrong one." "That man/woman of God missed God this time." Sometimes we just feel too accomplished, because no one in our family has come this far before, and so we settle for the less that God did not intend for us to stop at. When we do that, we are shooting for less than the bulls-eye of God's will, and sometimes He'll allow us to walk in that permissive will, but that's not His best for us. That was the case in Numbers chapters 13 and 14 when Moses sent out the spies to search out the land. Ten out of twelve of them came back with a bad report that said, *"the land is good, but we will not be able to take it because we were like grasshoppers in our own eyes when we compared the people of the land to us."*

They had become complacent in occupying the land that God promised His servant Abraham, and so there was no inspiration to go and take their rightful possession, and we all know how serious God takes His promises. They had spent too much time in Kadesh Barnea where there were good sources of water, compared to the waters of the wilderness. They spent thirty-eight out of the forty years that they journeyed from Egypt to the Promised Land, in this place (Deut. 2:14). Therefore, God said that none of the people twenty years and older, except the two spies (Joshua and Caleb – Num. 32:11-13) who came with good reports, will enter the Promised Land. It was convenient for them for a moment, but it later cost them their destiny. That is a very dangerous place to be in God. Complacency really kills the desire for more of what God has for us.

But the "Enoch lifestyle" goes for all of God, and with God, it does not hit and miss. I know we have been programmed to believe that we cannot get it right the first time, but God wants us to get it right all of the time, so that we don't waste time wandering in our wilderness aimlessly. The wilderness is good, because it builds character in us, but we don't have to put up our tents and set up camp there for good. I believe that God is not holding things from us because He wants to punish us, but because He is waiting for us to grow to maturity, so that we cannot abuse the things that He has for us. This does not mean that if we miss God, He will not restore us back. He certainly will; however, being the type of Father that He is; He wants the best for us.

OUR ULTIMATE EXAMPLE

Someone may ask, "Well is Enoch greater than our father of faith – Abraham, or our ultimate example Jesus Christ? The answer is a definite no. Enoch came before Abraham, as well as many others too, but the God who does the choosing, chose Abraham to be our father of faith, and also to be the first seed of the genealogy of Jesus Christ (Matthew 1:2). It is interesting how Adam, who walked with God, was not in there, nor was Enoch or the other patriarchs; however, Hebrews 12:1 tells us that we are surrounded by a cloud of witnesses, and those witnesses are those who have gone before us, to give us a blueprint of how we should live. Enoch was one of those witnesses, and I believe that the Holy Spirit has a message about this prophet's life that He wants the Body of Christ to see. That is why He asked me to write this book. However, our ultimate example is the

Lord Himself. That is whom Enoch had to look to for the start and finish of his faith (Hebrews 12: 2), and that is whom we should look to. It will be foolish to think that we can do anything apart from Him, because without Him we are helpless. Therefore, the name "The Enoch Lifestyle" should not throw anyone off as giving glory to a man, but rather to the God whom he served.

It is simply an example of how we should live a life of faith, and not allow fear to dominate our lifestyle, because by doing this we will be powerless against the wiles of the devil. There is no weapon in the arsenal of the enemy that is more powerful than fear, but we have to realize that *God has not given us a spirit of fear, but of power, and of love, and of a sound mind* (2 Timothy 1:7).

THE NATURE OF THE BEAST

There is nothing new under the sun, as Ecclesiastes 1:9 states. The old serpent has no new tricks in the hat. If we go back to the Word of God, we will find out how he operates. He still uses his three main divisions of sin that he used against our Lord in the wilderness, after the Lord had fasted for forty days and forty nights (Luke 4:1-13). They are the lust of the flesh, the lust of the eyes, and the pride of life (1 John 2:16). There is no force in the universe that can pluck us out from under the protection of our God. Proverbs 18:10 tell us that:

"The name of the LORD is a strong tower; the righteous run to it and are safe."

That devil knows that there is nothing that can harm us if we stay in God, so he uses tricks and tactics to get us from under the protection of God, and if that does not work, he uses his best tool in all his arsenal; fear. To understand this better, one has to study the two animals that the Bible relates satan to. They are the *lion* and the *serpent*. Let us take a look at the character of these two animals to see why the Word of God singled them out.

THE SERPENT - The serpent is a very clever and careful animal, and in the spiritual, it represents the cunning craftiness of the devil. The Lord Himself told us to be *as wise as serpent*s (Matthew 10:16), and I believe that was why the enemy used that animal to tempt Eve.

"Now the serpent was more cunning than any beast of the field, which the LORD God had made. And he said to the woman, "Has God indeed said, 'You shall not eat of every tree of the garden'?" (Genesis 3:1)

Stealth is a snake's number one weapon of choice, and that is exercised through the cousin of wisdom – patience that the snake has in abundance. That ability is what gives it the wisdom that it has. Unlike other animals that have to eat everyday, a snake doesn't have to, so it uses that to its advantage of studying its prey. It will not immediately attack its victim, even if it sees that the victim is vulnerable. Even though it knows that its venom is highly toxic and it can kill its victim with a single strike, or in the case of a constrictor, overpower its victim by its strength, the snake will make sure that it does not put itself in danger first, before doing anything. That is why it can lie quietly in one spot and study the behavior of the animal it is about to attack, before making the attack. This is because when it attacks, it wants to surprise the victim and not miss. It makes sure that the victim is not aware of its presence, and most of the time the snake will catch its prey when the animal's defenses are down. This is exactly what the enemy, satan, does in luring his victims to sin, and to get them away from the presence of God.

As a child of God, he knows that you know a thing or two about his strategies, and so he tries to catch you when your defenses are down; when you are not in the Spirit. That is why we should not be ignorant of his devices. The "Enoch lifestyle" is definitely not ignorant about the enemy's devices.

The devil is not wise and after his fall, God has never attributed wisdom to his nature. There is only one place in the Word of God that mentions the wisdom of the devil and that is Ezekiel 28 verse 12, but that was before his fall. After that, all that is mentioned of the evil one is that he is crafty, the father of lies, comes as an angel of light, and so on. The reason why you need to note that is because his strategies are still the same. He tempts us to bring us out from under the protection of God to a place where we are vulnerable, and then strikes. What he has is an understanding of the nature of man, having exploited with our weaknesses for thousands of years. He, through patience, will try to get us out from under the protection of God with the same temptations, but with different ways of appeal. He was in Eden when God created man, and because he was jealous of us, he found a way to get the first Adam to fall; ever since, he has been using the same old tactics. Please note that the serpent is not the devil. That animal was used by the evil one, because of its cunning nature, to tempt the woman in the Garden of Eden (Genesis 3). In Mathew 10:16, the Lord tells us to be as wise as serpents, and to me that is another way God shows his disregard for the devil, by associating wisdom to the animal (the serpent and not the devil) that he used to tempt, and get man out of the plan of God. Never will you find in God's Word a mention of the wisdom of satan, because he has none.

You see, the "Enoch lifestyle" realizes that true wisdom is a spirit (Isaiah 11:2) that only God can give (Proverbs 2:6), and so it trusts in God for that wisdom. That type of wisdom is spontaneous and does not rely on manipulation or trickery, which is what the enemy uses. You can relate satan's tricks to a doctor's probe for an ailment in your body (please note that the doctor is not the devil). The doctor gives you a questionnaire that asks you a bunch of questions, and based on your reply, the doctor makes an intelligent guess that your condition is this or that. That is done even before you do tests to confirm his/her assumptions (that is why they are given a license to practice on you). The devil knows your likes and dislikes, and so he tempts you with what he feels will draw you out from under your covering. Just like the doctor does not know your condition, except by your answer on that questionnaire, satan really does not know if you will fall to that temptation. He does not know if you have matured and overcome that area of weakness in your life. It is your answers (your speech) that give him a clue as to what you are most vulnerable to.

In reality, you have matured and do have the ability to overcome that temptation in your life. A good analogy I heard from a preacher at a leadership seminar to prove that you have is this: [1]"A man went backstage to see the animals that had just finished performing at a circus. All of a sudden, he got scared when he saw that the elephants were not restrained, or in cages and went back to the trainer to tell him that he didn't think it was safe to be out there with the animals alone. The trainer went back there with the man and told him, "Oh you don't need to be afraid, they are restrained." The man looked at the trainer in confusion, not knowing what he was talking about. Then the trainer showed him a flimsy rope around the elephant's leg and explained to the man, "When these animals were little guys, we tied this rope around their legs and anchored it to something strong. They tried all they could to get out of it, but because they were little, they didn't have the strength to get out of it. They kept on trying, but since they couldn't get out of it, they eventually gave up. Now anytime that rope is around their leg, they think that they are restrained." The elephant does not even have to use a quarter of its 15,000 pounds to free itself, but it can't, because its mind feels it still has that same baby strength. Albert Einstein made it plain for us. He said, [2] *"You can never solve a problem on the level on which it was created."*

Child of God, for you the great thing is that your mind is already developed. You just have walk in your full potential now.

THE LION – I must admit I was a little bit reserved when considering relating the character of the devil to that of the lion, because the lion is one of my favorite animals, and also because the lion is directly related to our Lord as the Lion of the tribe of Judah (Revelations 5:5). However, the difference is that our Lord *is* the Lion of the tribe of Judah, while the devil, as usual, is the pretender.

"Be sober, be vigilant; because your adversary the devil walks about like a roaring lion, seeking whom he may devour." (1 Peter 5:8)

Unlike the serpent, a lion does not rely much on stealth to hunt, as it is a very strong animal and can overpower its victims quickly by its strength. It is not called the king of the jungle for nothing. It is not afraid of any beast; basically, it is not afraid to fight. Proverbs 30:30 tells us that this animal does not turn down a fight. It walks about with the mentality of a king. It is not as big and strong as the elephant, nor is it as fast as the cheetah. The giraffe has it beat for height, and it is not even known for its wisdom. That honor is reserved for the snake, but one thing that the lion has that no other beast can challenge is its confidence, which makes it carry itself like the king of all beasts. But no description of this big cat is complete without the mention of its majestic roar. Some reports state that the roar of the lion can be heard up to five kilometers away. That roar is what sends fear into other animals and makes them so terrified of the big cat. According to scientists, pound for pound, the lion is not even the strongest animal in the wild, but the roar, backed up with an aggressive nature, makes it hard to challenge.

That roar is what the enemy imitates to bring fear to a lot of believers, especially if he sees that the believer is not going to fall for his tricks when he assumes the nature of the snake. He does not have the authority of the Lion of the tribe of Judah, so instead, he imitates it. The roar can come in many areas of life, such as financial crises, disappointments, or the death of a loved one. He has used it all through history, but the people who understood it have always prevailed against him. It is no secret that if you ignore his plan of seducing you out of the will of God by temptation, that he will come at you with that roar to try and intimidate you. In those tough times in the midst of the roars, he will whisper lies that you will never make it out of that situation, but we know the truth. If God brought you out in those other times, you can guarantee that He will do it again. You can always guarantee that if you set your mind in going to the other side of God's plan for your life, he will not let you go without a real test. He tried that with the Lord in Luke 8: 21-25 when He got to the boat to go to the other side of the lake. He brought a storm to stop the Lord from getting to His destination, but the reaction of the Lord is what I believe every child of God should have. He had so much peace that the winds and the waves beating into the boat did not bother him to the point of interrupting his sleep. He only woke up when His disciples woke Him up, which is a demonstration that of how insignificant the problem is if you have God on your side. The "Enoch lifestyle" is really that type of child-like faith, which relies wholly on God, regardless of the situation.

So don't see it as something strange; he has asked permission from your Father to tempt you, as he did for Peter (Luke 22:31) and Job (Job 1:6-12). The interesting thing is that your Father has allowed him to test you, so as to prove you, which will eventually make you stronger and prove to that devil that your elder brother Jesus Christ has given you the victory over him. No matter what nature (the one of the snake or of the lion) he uses to come at you, the end goal is simple; to get you to doubt the word that God gave you and put you in a state of fear, which is the enemy of faith. That is why Psalm 91:13 tells us that we will trample the lion and the adder. If he succeeds in getting you to the point of fear, then he has succeeded in crippling you and made you powerless. Therefore, he will no longer fear what you say or do, because he knows that you are not saying or doing it in faith. That is the state that most of the Church of Jesus Christ is in now, and as long as we stay on that side of the fence, we will not succeed in doing the will of God. However, that does not have to be the case with us, as Jesus has paid the price on Calvary for us to have and operate in total victory. As I said earlier, if Enoch conquered by his faith, we can too and we can learn from this great patriarch how he did it. If it is through faith that we please God, and without it we cannot please Him, then this faith thing should be a way of life, instead of sporadic last resort calls when all else has failed.

We don't need to be afraid of the strategies of the evil one. There is no trick that he can pull out of his filthy bag of tricks that the Word of God has no solution for. He is not even a lion, as the 1 Peter 5:8 scripture states. He only is pretending to have the resolve of the true Lion of the tribe of Judah, who is our Lord Jesus Christ. Every type of sin that he tries to lure you into, whether it is one of lust, or of lack of faith in God, is for one purpose, and that is to cut you off from communication with your heavenly Father, so that you can miss Him when He is trying to direct you. But don't be afraid of him. Psalm 91:13 tell us that we will trample the lion and the adder under our feet. That is his address and the only place that fits him. My desire is that anyone who picks up "The Enoch Lifestyle", that faith will start to well up in them to the point that as they read this book, they will realize the power and authority that they have in Christ.

CHAPTER 2

THE CAUSE

GET OUT OF THE CLOSET

We are living in a time where men seek to gain recognition through their pain by whatever means possible, even if that means giving up their life for it. Never in the history of mankind have there been so many people willing to die for a cause, as in the 20th and 21st centuries, and it seems like it really doesn't matter what the cause is. In the wake of the 9/11 attacks in the US, the common question asked amongst citizens around the world was not why the attacks were carried out, but how the terrorists broke through our defenses. The question 'why' was not even an issue, after it was established that the attacks were not the result of aeronautical error, but were deliberate actions by Al-Qaida terrorists. It is not a secret that Al-Qaida is a radical terror group that seeks to get attention by hitting key areas of interests in the world, no matter what the cost of lives is to them or the victims. Everyone knew what he or she stood for, and that *they* needed the world to be aware of their presence

In his own words, Seung-Hui Cho, who killed 32 people in the shooting spree on the Virginia Tech campus on 16 April 2007, said,

[3]"You thought it was one pathetic boy's life you were extinguishing. Thanks to you, I die like Jesus Christ, to inspire generations of the weak and the defenseless people." Everyone wants to be heard, and if they feel like their pain is being ignored, they will go all out to get that attention. Extremists don't mind being martyred for what they believe in, as long as they contribute to a cause that dramatically alters the course of history, regardless of how significant the thing is.

If you have given your life to the Lord and are living for Him, you are not exempt from this group of extremists. You have been called everything from A to Z in the book, but the normal ones. Some people think that we are one of the most out of touch people on the face of the earth, saying that Jesus Christ is the only way to heaven and no one else. Some simply think that there is just a chemical imbalance in us. We know the truth to that, and it is that we are peculiar people that are in this world, but not of this world. My question then is this: Why do we seek to live otherwise? We have one foot in the will of the Lord and the other in the will of the world. That in-between type of lifestyle is not how Enoch came to please God. He was all for pleasing God and no one else.

This Enoch type of lifestyle is not going to get any easier in these days. Society is becoming more and more tolerant with a lot of things that it used to frown upon. Same-sex unions, pornography, dysfunctional families where either father or mother is absent, (which is the result of the breakdown of family values) and even the new fling lifestyle, adopted by married couples, where married couples would meet and have sex with each other's spouses without any after act obligations just to satisfy their lust, are not new under the sun. However, what's new about it in our generation is the general acceptance of such lifestyles of the general public. Let's remember, before we forget that God took out a whole city for that type of general acceptance of sin (Genesis 19).

Everyone is out of the closet but believers. While we are having our pity party about what God has or has not yet done, and the other half of us putting on a good show of intellectual dominance, there is a secret warfare being waged on us to strip us of any freedom that we are enjoying now. You may ask what freedom? A good example is the airing of Christian TV, which is so hated by liberals that they would do anything to stop it if they can, but how can they stop something that is born of God (1 John 5:4)? We believers tend to be so passive in relation to our faith. The rest of the world has captured the revelation that for any course of action to fully take root and be taken seriously, one has to be sold out and be prepared to go all the way, even if it means losing their lives. No one wants to be identified with any movement whose members are not sure if they want to be in it or not. Everyone wants to belong to a cause that is sure of what it stands for, and whose members are confident about what they believe in. We don't have a mere movement; we have the business of the Kingdom of God, but until we start to believe in it to the point of giving our lives for it, it will not affect lives the way it should.

Many people can remember the "gay pride" movement in the US that took everyone by surprise. They achieved their goal, because they persisted, even though it came about through much persecution, which included them losing some lives. But thinking of that kind of persistence, or if I may call it "reckless abandonment of personal safety", you don't have to look far to find that in history. The scriptures tell us that our very faith was founded and sustained on that principle. Jesus says in Matthew 10:39 that if you keep your life you will lose it, but if you lose it you'll find it. He exemplified that by laying down His own life for us, and most of the disciples followed that noble example.

THERE'S A WAR GOING ON

Child of God, we enlisted in the Lord's Army at a time of war, and the enemy will not hold back because of our pretty banners that warn him to stay in his own sector, because we are God's children. The phrase 'peace-time' does not exist in God's vocabulary as it relates to making truce with the devil. That might sound too extreme for a lot of folks, but we do that everyday in our lethargy towards the things of God. Our indifference indeed speaks volumes, and it comes out loud and clear to the other side as truce seekers. In the military, we are taught to "never surrender at our own free will" to the enemy, and that is the warrior ethos for all US soldiers. If you do that, you are considered a defector, and can be charged with treason if caught. Now there is a very important lesson we should learn from that, even though that is a physical thing. We are never to be so in tune with this world's system that we start to embrace its way of doing things. Paul says that we are in this world, but not of the world. That means we ultimately don't belong here, and by embracing the ways of this passing world, we may lose sight of our goal, which is to bring glory to the Father.

In April of 2003 when my unit marched into Baghdad following Bradley tanks and the infantry, we were armed to the teeth, not taking anything for granted. We were a regular aviation support battalion that was not accustomed to the irregularities of urban warfare, but that didn't keep the enemy from attacking us. They realized that as long as we were wearing the uniform that identifies us as US troops, we were qualified as prime targets; therefore, they didn't care what branch of service we were, but did everything they could to kill, capture, or maim anyone they could. Therefore, we came ready to the battlefield.

Unfortunately, many of us believers are not taking this warfare serious enough. We have a 'whatever' type of attitude when it comes to it, but our enemy is serious about it, and will do anything to stop us from advancing the Kingdom of God, because he knows that his days are short and numbered. If you call yourself a believer, and believe in the cleansing blood that flowed freely from our Lord's side, make no mistake about it, the battle cry has been sounded and the battle-axe is swinging high in the air, aiming for the neck of the church. We cannot afford to be passive in this fight anymore. Our silence is costing us the loss of territory, but we can get it back if we are ready.

GOOD WORKS

The main reason a lot of believers are so lethargic about the things of God is that they have left off from doing the works of God, and have been consumed by mere "good works" (church work). Work is good, but when the Holy Spirit is not present in it, it becomes hard and very burdensome. Then it becomes a struggle, and folks in that predicament become disillusioned, disgruntled, and hard to get along with. We should never forget that it is the Holy Spirit who makes the difference. He is the one who brings the anointing that breaks the yoke or burden. A lot of us have not tapped into the presence of God to have a real experience with His Shekinah glory. Sad to say, apart from the occasional goose bumps that we experience on a Sunday morning worship service, a lot of us don't wait in His presence long enough to experience the overflow. We don't wait long enough for instructions, but just follow the high we had from the last experience, and guess our way through to the next step.

Many a time, the Holy Spirit, who should guide us into every truth, is long gone, but we are stuck at a step, because of the experience of past glories, all in the name of "our fathers did it like that." Good works are good, but only if the Holy Spirit initiated them. If He didn't, then we are in religion, rather than a relationship. Religion is man made and does not touch God. It is man's desperate way of reaching God, while relationship is man reaching out to God. Religion is really dead works; it kills.

THE DIFFERENCE

JEREMIAH 6:16

"Thus says the Lord: Stand in the ways and see, and ask for the old paths, where the good way is, and walk in it; Then you will find rest for your souls. But they said, 'We will not walk in it.'"

PSALM 78: 14

"In the daytime also He led them with the cloud, and all the night with a light of fire."

There is an old path that the Lord has prescribed for His children to walk in, and that is what Jeremiah 6:16 is talking about. It is the path of righteousness, and though it may be unpopular at times, if followed, the end results are far rewarding than the shortcut of sinful pleasures. Jesus Himself has told us in Matthew 7:13 that the road is narrow that leads to eternal life. That is why it doesn't bother me when people call me close-minded for the Kingdom's sake. As my pastor (W.J. Moreland) would say, *"you have to be close-minded to please God."* There is one way and not many others to the Father, and that way to Him is narrow. That way is His Son Jesus Christ. It is that way that God was telling us about in Psalm 11:3 that if the foundations are destroyed what can the righteous do? The answer to that is nothing, because we cannot build on another foundation other than Christ. That old path is what the Holy Spirit wants us to stand upon, and not church doctrines and man made regulations that give no revelation of the Son of God. You see, regulations tend to control the move of the Spirit in your life, while a revelation exposes the nuggets of God's truth and propels you a step, or steps higher in God. That is where we miss it, because we tend to spend a lot of time on where the Spirit was a year or generations ago, instead of where He is leading us to now. That is the reason we have a lot of denominations and divisions in the body of Christ today. A lot of us just find it right to believe in something different, and everyone is fighting for the preservation of their ministry, and not so much for the proclamation of the Gospel of Jesus Christ, but from the beginning it was not so.

Before Jesus was crucified, He prayed to the Father for the church that we become one as He and the Father are one. We, as a body, are not united as He intended yet. I say 'yet', because the Holy Spirit is not done with us yet. He is still in the business of uniting the church, and as Jesus prayed; we will see it fulfilled.

After we have asked for the old paths, and have started walking in them, then can the Holy Spirit lead us by His cloud at daytime and fire by night time. You see, the old paths are the foundation of the Gospel of Jesus as I stated above; therefore, when any believer of

Christ is grounded in the foundations of the gospel, what he/she is saying is that they are now ready for the Holy Spirit to lead them. Parents understand it better by this analogy; how can we reward our children, or trust them with a greater task if they did not obey the last instruction that we gave them. Likewise, how can the Spirit lead us if we are still being led by the lust of the eyes, flesh, and the pride of life? That is why it is very important to be grounded in the elementary principles of Christ (Hebrews 6:1-2), so that we can build a foundation upon that.

Therefore, we see from Jeremiah 6:16 that we need to be grounded in the ways of the Lord, so that we can be led of His Spirit, as stated in Psalm 78: 14. This is what keeps us from becoming stagnant and refusing to move when the Spirit wants to move on.

GOD LOVES 'HIDE AND SEEK'

If there is any kid game God loves to play, I strongly believe it is the game of hide and seek. He takes pleasure in His children seeking Him, and He loves to hide. This is not because He wants us to be frustrated in looking for Him, but because He has established a law that everything that is precious must be sought after with diligence. It is in the pursuit of that valuable thing (in this case our relationship with Him) that we become transformed into His image. Two scriptures confirm my assumption. Isaiah says of Him:

ISAIAH 45:15

"Truly You are God, who hide Yourself, O God of Israel, the Savior!"

ISAIAH 55:6

"Seek the LORD while He may be found, Call upon Him while He is near."

The "Enoch lifestyle" realizes this and sees it as a privilege to seek God. The plan and purpose of God for mankind is so huge that it will literally give us a nervous breakdown if He reveals all of it to us. That is why He breaks it down in segments and by individual members of His church, so that there will always be a need to come back to Him for further instructions, after a segment is complete. It also creates a need for us to be in His presence, so that we will depend on His strength to carry out His instructions, rather than our own selves. That is why He told the children of Israel not to store the manna from heaven, or else it would stink. He was telling them that even though the anointing was good and got them through yesterday's battle, that they could not use the same anointing for today's battle, because they would miss God, which they ended up doing anyway.

In Psalm 78:14, two things grabbed my attention, and I paid close attention to them, so that I wouldn't miss out on the revelation that was being given to me at the moment. Those two things were the words 'cloud' and 'light of fire.' These subjects in this complex sentence were carefully chosen by the Holy Spirit (as He did with every word He chose to use in the scriptures). Clouds are very unpredictable. They can be very tricky in weather forecasting. In Meteorology, (the science dealing with the atmosphere and its phenomena, including weather and climate) it is the instability of the atmosphere that produces clouds, and not the other way around. The more unstable the atmosphere is, the more severe the weather could be. Clouds and storms are formed when pockets of air rise and cool, as they expand in the lower portion of the upper atmosphere, which if related to the move of the Spirit, is the sign that the Spirit has moved. That is why in the book of Exodus whenever the clouds moved; it was a sign to the children of Israel to move.

Most church leaders and saints don't like to stir the root of religious orders, and would rather die for an organization than for the principles of the doctrines of Christ. They would be surprised to find out that the glory cloud left a long time ago, and this they would know if they had inquired from the One who guides the church – The Holy Spirit. It is indeed a very sad state to be in as the Spirit can be leading, but because you are no longer sensitive to His leading, you miss Him completely. This was what happened to the religious leaders in Jesus' time. They kept on looking for the Messiah, even after He came and left, and missed God completely. They were stuck at a step, expecting God to bring His king in a spectacular fashion and style. As Jesus said, they were blind guides leading the blind; blocking the way to the Kingdom of Heaven, while they themselves refused to enter in. A lot of people today blame those leaders for acting the way they did, exempting themselves from such actions as were typical of the Jews in those days. But believe this, if Jesus came in our time, He would face the same criticism, or more that He faced from the Jews. Religious people will still be trying to stop Him from associating with the prostitutes and drug lords, and would still be trying to make His Gospel a political or religious one, instead of to all. I We see it all the time; people removing Christ, or the anointed One, out of the message in something as simple as Christmas, rather than making it a 'Christ to all the masses' message.

Fire is another property that the Holy Ghost likes to use to describe the thermal state of the Church in the Word of God. Fire, as we all know produces light. During the exodus of the children of Israel, God was their sufficiency, and as long as they followed Him, there was no need for another source of light. As a matter of fact, they did not need any form of navigation system, because the Holy Ghost, who moved on the shapeless face of the earth and formed it into what it is today, was with them. All they had to do was follow His leading by going where the fire led. Fire always refers to temperature in the Word, and it can either be constructive or destructive. Whether it is talking about the Lord our God being a consuming fire (Deuteronomy 4:24), or of it being used as a sign of welcome (Acts 28:4), there is always some form of heat being produced or anticipated by its application. This is seen all throughout the Word of God, and I strongly believe that is why the Holy Ghost used it so much. However, just like clouds, it can be very unstable and just as easy as it can light up a house with its brightness and benefit many with its illumination, so can it set ablaze the same house and burn it down to the ground.

Jesus told the people in Matthew 6:23, "If therefore the light that is in you is darkness how great is that darkness." That is because when we stop following the brightness of the fire of the Holy Ghost and start using other supplements, we automatically turn our light into darkness. He is the only light that we need and will ever need. God showed His displeasure of that in Numbers 3:4 when Nadab and Abihu offered strange or profane fire before Him. They died before Him, leaving no seed (children) to carry their names.

The Holy Spirit, being the gentleman that He is, will not force us to receive anything that He revealed. That is why you see a greater demonstration of the power of God in developing countries, and a lesser impact in the developed ones. Their fire is burning bright. When we, in developed, industrial nations, are forcing God out of our public places, they are accepting Him. But this I know, your fire will never go out if you can only keep the desire for His presence at the hunger level, and never allow it to dip to the snacking level and that is the "Enoch lifestyle." The overflow of His Shekinah glory is what the "Enoch lifestyle" needs to influence the world. In the overflow of His presence, there are blessings and breakthroughs. It is a matter of common sense. How can you testify of something that you haven't experienced? But O, that we could stay long enough to see just His finger. It is impossible to experience a touch of God and remain the same. Experience in this sense is not the acknowledgement of Jesus Christ as your Lord and Savior and the repentance from dead works (Hebrews 6:1). It is what we have to go through to become a son. We are being changed from a child who has not much of a right to the promises than a slave, to Sons of God, and thus heirs to the Father through Christ (Galatians 4: 1-7). But as long as we remain children, we will never enjoy those privileges. That is the level that a lot of Christians stay at until they see the Father's face.

When we decide to find God after we have been gone from Him for a while, we should not expect Him in the same place where we left Him. He may have moved. That is what I mean by God loves the 'hide and seek' game. His principles of righteousness, holiness, and a hunger for Him will remain the same, but He may have changed the order of service on you (as a figure of speech). He may have you do the praise and worship before the announcements, or vice versa. But if you are always following Him, you'll always know when He changes things around. I also believe that the deep things of God are only revealed when He sees that He has our attention. This can be seen in Ex. 3:4. It is when He saw that the bush caught Moses' attention that He started to reveal more to him. If you don't think His agenda is important, and you have time for everything but Him, He may never reveal His deep secrets to you.

I strongly believe that we are at the cusp of the curve where power, influence, and the perishable wealth of this evil generation is going to shift from the people who don't know God, to the ones who are known by God, as His sons (mind you this can mean both male and female). The Psalmist says in Psalm 126:1-3 that when God turned around the captivity of Zion, it was like them that dreamed. They were so overwhelmed with joy that it burst out into laughter, so much so that the people of the nations (ones that didn't know God, or rather weren't known of God) took notice, and said that indeed God has done great things for them. Get ready friends, these are the last days. God will be doing such great and marvelous things, that the ones who don't know Him will be really surprised.

CHAPTER 3

TOTAL DOMINION OVER (GANGS)

There is a battle being waged not only in the inner cities of America, but in every major metropolitan city of the world that most people prefer not to talk about, hoping it will go away by ignoring it, or by just being neutral about it. But in the midst of that silence, lives are being taken violently and the cities ravaged. The innocent can only watch helplessly as their young and old are forcefully taken out of this world, some maimed for life. The fear of being "taken out" by the perpetrators of these crimes, keep the innocent who know any information about a crime hushed as the code "you snitch, you die" is fully enforced in these communities. Children in these communities, as young as five, have seen violent crimes being committed, but the code has to be enforced, so the older ones tell them to hush.

You should know by now exactly who I am talking about. Well, if you don't, let me introduce you to the world of gangs, the silent rulers of the inner cities of the world that is, if we let them. Just like terrorists they work silently, but fearlessly, determined to spread their control by recruiting young members who instill fear into their victims through the way they commit their senseless crimes. They will stop at nothing short of their ultimate goal, which is total dominance. There is a reason why they want this dominion established so badly. It is so that they can control the flow of illegal money in any community.

Gangs have been in existence from the foundations of civilization, and have influenced the way people lived in one way or the other. They have always been ruthless and violent and interestingly, have always had some form of public support in one way or another. However, there is one thing about gangs and society that should be a cause for concern to anyone that is listening. That is that gangs have all of a sudden become cool all around the world in the past fifteen or so years, and the culture is so deeply embedded in our societies that it really doesn't matter where one is in the world; the message that is portrayed comes across loud and clear: You can dress fly (nice) and live large, but you don't have to have a good work ethic, or rather a legitimate income to do that. The emphasis is to acquire as much material assets as you can to parade your worldly successes that the other guy or kid, whose single parent is trying to put food on the table for him/her, has a challenge in obeying that parent.

The gangster lifestyle is glorified in almost all of media, and the kids are the victims. Most clothing lines and the entertainment media don't even know that they are a medium for that type of lifestyle (make no mistake about it – some know, but just don't care). They target the young crowd whose whole lifestyle is centered on entertainment and fashion, and just can't do without the hoopla of who or what's hot now. That's why you always hear them asking, "Have you checked out the latest this or that? Parents get caught up in the actions too. However, while we parents go for what is cool or is in fashion, there is another system of values going on in our very homes and in the minds of our young ones.

THE MISCONCEPTION

In all of this, there is a great misconception amongst Christians, and that is that the government of any nation is responsible to get rid of gangs in the various communities that they are affecting. While it is true that the Bible admonishes us to pray for the peace of the city where we live that we may live a peaceful and quiet life, (1Timothy 2:1,2), (Jeremiah 29: 7), there is another responsibility that we Christians have, but don't seem to acknowledge. This might be due to the lack of knowledge of the facts, which eventually results in fear. That responsibility is to rule on this earth as God originally intended when He gave Adam that charge in Genesis 1: 29, 30.

And God said, "See I have given you every herb that yields seed which is on the face of the earth, and every tree whose fruit yields seed; to you it shall be for food. Also, to every beast of the earth, to every bird of the air, and to every thing that creeps on the earth, in which there is life, I have given every green herb for food": and it was so.

This is the charge that was given to us by our God, and it is the realm where every man or woman walking in the Enoch type of faith or lifestyle should aspire to live. While others are crying and complaining about what God has or has not done, and blaming Him for the evils that are happening in the world (even through gang violence), the Enoch type of lifestyle is not moved, regardless of what happens. He/she does not know God by His acts, but by His ways, just as He showed His acts to the children of Israel, but His ways to Moses (Psalm 103: 7), because Moses had a relationship with Him. So when evil happens, that man or woman will not align that with God, because he/she knows the nature and character of God. They know that He is always in the business of doing good things, and that His intention for mankind is only good.

However, what has happened is that we have given our authority away, and are blaming God for everything that is happening in the world, together with everyone. In the process, we have exchanged roles. Rather than being the city on the hill that has this wonderful effect of attracting people to it because of its beauty and strategic position for times of refuge, we have lowered our standards so low that we are now in the valleys looking for refuge. This is because we have not searched the word to find out what the Father left in the will for us. We all know that no one can benefit from something they don't know about. We have been covetous of the stranger's kid's fancy toys that the kid has been parading to show how good it is to have a dad as his, but our Daddy wrote in the will that the toy store carrying the toys and all of the toys belong to us. We should not be surprised if the other side looks attractive and makes us want to go over and play for a little while, which really will eventually make us stay over there. It is because we haven't searched the will, which is God's Word, and so ignorance is costing us more than we can afford. It is costing us our lives, plus the lives of our generations to come, and that is just because we refuse to find out what was left for us in the will. Ignorance will always produce fear, because of uncertainty of what will happen when you are about to take a step forward, and that is the state that the body of Christ is at now.

Note that I said "we" in referring to the body of Christ. That's because the body is one, and the Lord is coming for one unified body and not bits and pieces of us, so while some of us are doing well, the others are still lacking and until we all are ready, we will delay the coming of our soon coming King. Please note this:

GOD HAS NO ONE BUT HIS CHILDREN TO PUT THE DEVIL BACK IN HIS PLACE AND BRING HIS KINGDOM BACK ON EARTH.

So, while we cry about the injustices of life and blame God for all of it, know that the heavens where many of us are striving to get to, to avoid all of our sorrows, belong to God. It is the earth that He has given to the sons of men (Psalm 115: 16). This is not to say that we should not look forward to being with Him in heaven; however, while we are here let's rule, and in ruling let's have ourselves a good time in doing that too. We have a guaranteed ticket to heaven (excuse my analogy); let's stop striving to get there. We will be coming back to the earth with the Lord to rule, so why not start practicing now.

SAY SOMETHING

The Enoch type of life is not and will not live in fear. It refuses to. That lifestyle turns wimps into champions. The person living that lifestyle doesn't see him/herself as a victim or a survivor, but always as the overcomer. If you try to put him/her down, they will always look for a way up and will always rise up above their oppressors, because the God of that type of lifestyle is one who knows no defeat. That is why it is imperative that we realize the authority that is available to us. Believe it or not, if you are a believer, you have the authority and power to stop gang activity in your neighborhood. It is not the government's fault that gangs are prevalent in metropolitan cities. It is because we are not taking our rightful authority. I am not saying that we have to go out there and battle *"mano-a-mano"* with gangs. Then, that will be a physical fight. We do not fight against flesh and blood, but against principalities, against powers, against rulers of the darkness of this age, and against spiritual hosts of wickedness in the heavenly places (Ephesians 6:12). That is the type of warfare that we have in our hands.

We believers have yet to discover the power in our tongues. Our words are extremely important, even more than we can even imagine. That is why we cannot allow evil forces that operate through gangs to continue to impose their wills on our neighborhoods, while we just sit down and watch. How many rapes, murders, and drive-by shootings have to happen before we realize that we have the power to stop them? The elements of this physical world were created by words. Therefore, words are the only thing that the forces that control this physical world can listen to. I am not talking of vain babblings and repetitions, but of the confession through God's word of what we desire to see happening around us. A lot of what we call positive confessions in the body of Christ is actually just vain repetitions and hoping. That is why a lot of times we don't receive what we confess. *Real confession is passionate and the confessor is moved by his/her convictions from the realm of believing, to that of fully knowing.* Regardless of how bad your neighborhood is, there is still hope for it. If God has not given up on it, you shouldn't either. He has said that the words that come out of His mouth will not return to Him without accomplishing that thing that He sent it to accomplish (Isaiah 55:11). The men and women in a community are who make that community what it is. God never gives up on any one. They are very important to God, and until He tells them, "depart from me you workers of iniquity", we have no reason to give up.

We are charged to say something all throughout the Word of God. If God created the entire universe by saying something (Genesis

1), how do we figure that we can do it differently? The world was created by speech, and speech is the only thing it can respond to. If gang activity is infesting your neighborhood, and the situation is like a mountain that refuses to move, then speak to the demons that are controlling the young men and women in those gangs (Mark 11: 23, 24). Believe that what you say will happen, even if nothing that you prayed for has been seen by you yet. Everyone starts at a certain level, and so if you are at that level, instead of saying "what a shame" when you hear the bad report, start to speak against it, and tell those demons to leave your AO (Area of Occupation) in the name of our elder brother Jesus Christ. Serve them an ejectment notice and refuse to back down until you regain your territory, and you will know that when the violence ceases. That is why intercessory prayer is also necessary (I talk about that in the last chapter). Gangs love to claim territory. That is because the demon that controls them loves to claim territory that doesn't belong to him, and will do anything to gain control, so that it can expand its dominion.

The power to accomplish anything in God doesn't come from you, so please quit looking at yourself for the solution. In your best state, you by yourself are like a piece of paper at the mercy of a category 5 hurricane when facing the devil. However, the story always changes when you include your elder brother Jesus Christ in the equation. Therefore, I admonish you: Do not be afraid of them; your God has told you that every land that the soles of your feet tread upon shall be yours (Deuteronomy 11:24). That means that land that you are standing on now. The devil knows that you (a son of God) are in the area, and so he is doing all he can to run you off, because your prayers are bothering him and hindering his operations. Trust me; this is more effective than the police, highflying banners, and demonstrations (even though they too have their place). When you see them backing down, something on the inside of you will leap for joy, and your faith will start growing. You don't have to fight the enemy with his own weapons, because your own weapons are by far, way more effective.

IS IT GOD'S FAULT?

A lot of people, including believers, blame God for the evil that is happening in the world, and even question Him why He is not doing anything about it. Also, some people will say that if God is this almighty and all-powerful God, why doesn't He stop it? Well the answer to that is that He has given the earth to us, and as such, He is waiting for us to take dominion over the works of the devil (scripture). The main reason why nothing happens when a lot of believers pray or take authority is that they wait too long to prepare for the battle. We have to get out of the habit of having prayer meetings only when something goes wrong. By then, the forces that established the evil have intensified their powers and since we are not ready, it will be difficult to trust God for his power to show up. This is when we hear from even believers that the word of God does not work (in so many other words of course).

Whereas, if we stay grounded in the word and prayer, the angels go to work for us even before trouble knocks on our door, and when we speak they respond to voice of the word of God (Psalm 103:20) in our speech, and that is when things happen. This goes beyond speaking the word of God, because anyone can do that. The voice of the word that has the resolve of Psalm 29 comes from hiding the word of God richly in your spirit through meditation, and that goes past your favorite ten scriptures you first learned when you got saved. Without faith, as Hebrews 11:6 states, it is impossible to please God. If we don't believe our own prayers, then it is not God's fault for that. The responsibility of preparing for battle is on us, not God. He has given us the weapons. We have to use them now. Even nature itself teaches us that we are to take a stand. Isaac Newton's first law of motion states that every body will continue in its state of motion or rest, until it is acted upon by another force. Gang activity will continue in its state of motion until we put an end to it. The "Enoch lifestyle" sees the evil, and does something about it.

PERSISTENCE THAT PRODUCES RESULTS

Please beware. There is one principle satan uses to break down the feeble minded saints all the time. He adds this principle to his bag of tricks, and the combo works wonders. That principle is persistence. In Luke 18: 1 – 8, Jesus narrated the parable of the woman who refused to give up because of a little obstacle. She wanted justice from her adversary, but the problem was that the judge who was supposed to handle her case was a man who did not fear God, nor regarded the opinions of man. The woman who was a widow wasn't about to give up, as her husband was dead and probably had no one to go to. She made up her mind that she was going to wear out the judge's patience and it paid off for her, as she got her request from the judge who had refused her. Persistence is a tool that will work wonders if used correctly. The enemy has been using it on us for too long, but it is about time to turn the tables, and cause him to eat from the loser's side. Let us take the fight right up his alley, and see how he likes being cornered.

That tool of persistence has brought down governments, broken down partitions of walls, and even bridged the racial barriers of segregation. Some great examples are the falling of the Berlin wall, the breaking of the back of racial injustice in America by the civil rights movement, spearheaded by Dr. Martin Luther King Jr. and others, and even Nelson Mandela's commitment in spending twenty-seven years in prison for the liberation of his people from apartheid (as we all know, he later became the president of S. Africa after his time in prison). All of these people displayed persistence and a strong commitment to their cause, and some even their lost lives. Think about it saints, why can't it work for us in the fight against gang violence? We have to have a heart, and a determination that we are not going to tolerate it in our neighborhoods, but the fight will be won on our knees and in speaking the word of God about the situation – bringing the Kingdom to earth. We have been made kings and priests of the Almighty God, and where the word of the king is there is power (Ecclesiastes 8: 4), so say something about the situation. Refuse to back down from your beliefs.

The scriptures also state in Proverbs 18: 14 that the spirit of a man is what sustains him/her. If the spirit of a man is determined to fight through adversity, nothing can stop it. That is why the doctors of cancer patients can tell who has a fighting chance against the disease right from the time that person is diagnosed with it. If a patient gives up on him/herself, saying that the situation is hopeless, what happens is that since the body is neutral to both positive and negative thoughts, it starts to shut down, and most times the person does not make it. The positive person, on the other hand, refuses to accept those negative thoughts of death, and starts to send messages to the body through the subconscious that there is too much to live for; therefore, the body starts its healing process, instead of shutting down. Those types of people stand a better chance of surviving the disease, and go on to live for years to tell their victory against it. A very good example that comes to mind is [4]Lance Armstrong, who defeated testicular cancer and went on to win the Tour de France cycling competition from 1999 to 2005; a record seven consecutive victories that still stands.

Please read this quote by Calvin Coolidge, the 30th President of the United States:

[5]Nothing in the world can take the place of Persistence.

Talent will not; nothing is more common than unsuccessful people with talent.

Genius will not; unrewarded genius is almost a proverb.

Education will not; the world is full of educated derelicts.

Persistence and determination alone are omnipotent.

The slogan 'Press On' has solved and always will solve the problems of the human race.

Calvin Coolidge

30th President of US (1872 - 1933)

We have seen it all throughout history how the spirit of men gave them fighting chances against injustices, and prevailed against governments of tyranny. All of the above are good examples, but believe me, nothing in the history of mankind, or in the future of it, has more resolve than the power of God resident in every child of God. The Enoch type of life, the life of faith that pleases the Father, Son, and Holy Ghost, offers that type of victory against all adversity, and that includes gangs. Stand your ground in this fight of faith against those evil spirits of gang violence. Refuse to give up ground. They are the ones who will back down if we hold our ground. If we don't have a resolve in us to fight till the last ounce of energy is expended, then we stand no chance in this fight, because the enemy we are dealing with is determined to take this fight that far.

What will be our resolve? Are we going to back down every time and keep giving up territory until our backs are against the wall, or are we going to stand up and say "Enough is enough?" Maybe you have lost a family member to gang violence. Please go ahead and mourn them and let your tears flow freely. But remember, after the darkest part of the night, morning breaks. Don't allow that devil to keep you in that state forever. Pick up your weapons, and get busy. I have gone past belief on this subject, so therefore, I know that you reading this book can and will make a difference.

POWER OVER CREEPS

In the fight for our communities, our adversary is determined and will not go down without a fight. We should realize that we might have to come physically in contact with the perpetrators of gang activity, and face them eyeball-to-eyeball. If this happens, please don't back down. Before you shut me down, please answer this question for me. What is greater; the power of gangs, or the resident power of God in each believer? I know that they are violent and can deliver on their promise of death if you cross their path in a wrong way, and can also elude capture and prosecution for their crimes, but are we going to be afraid of someone that kills the body, but can't touch that which is eternal – your spirit? If so, then we may all lie down, so that we can get run over. Whether they are called Crips, Bloods, Mara Salvatrucha (MS-13), or any other, they have one thing in common, and that is that they all creep, and God has given you power over every creeping thing on the face of the earth (Genesis 1: 30). Creeping in gang vocabulary is to sneak up on the victim with the intent of surprising him/her, so that they will have little or no time to react; thereby, giving the attacker the advantage, just like a snake does in the hunt for its prey. Again, I am not telling you to place yourself in harm's way, because even Jesus' parents fled Judea being warned of an angel to go to Egypt (Matt 2:13). However, you don't have to be running from town to town seeking a safe neighborhood to live in if God has not sent you there. What you need to do is follow the leading of Holy Spirit for spiritual signals, and His voice. He will lead you into every truth. If He says go, then go. If He hasn't spoken, then don't move.

There is nothing that can surprise the man or woman living the Enoch type of life. This "Enoch lifestyle" is faith-filled and has no room for fear; faith has pushed all fear away; therefore, creepers are no surprise to him/her. This is because, as we in that type of lifestyle continually stay in the presence of God, we are being changed from glory to glory, and there is no option but to go from faith to faith. That is why the Holy Spirit is encouraging you through this little book right now to come over to this type of life, where you can [6]LIVE (Live In Victory Everyday). Like I asked earlier, why should we be afraid of someone that kills only the body, but can't touch the soul that lives forever? But I see it happening everyday, believers refusing to stand up against the violence in their communities, because of a flimsy fire arm or a knife. We see murders committed everyday, and look the other way just because somebody promised that if we snitch on them, we will pay for it with our lives. At the same time, the blood of the innocent is crying for justice. But it is not surprising why a whole lot of us are afraid to stand up against injustice. We do not have a history with God. David had one with Him, so when the Philistine showed up disrespecting his God, he knew immediately that his God would protect him from the giant, and He did.

THOSE WITH US ARE MORE THAN THOSE AGAINST US

God is not asking us to do anything that has not been done before, but even if that is the case, I love the sound of the word 'pathfinder' better than that of a 'follower'. All throughout the Word of God, we see the people who know their God doing great exploits for Him. In 2 Kings 6, a bunch of creeps, sent by their leader the king of Syria, crept up to the man of God Elisha's house at night wanting to capture him in the morning, and take him to their master. They did not know that they had walked in to a divine trap set for them. The cause of contention was that the king of Syria, who was at war with the king of Israel, was tired of his military plans he disclosed only to his top generals in his bedroom being leaked to the king of Israel. Whenever he came up with a strategy of how and where he was going to attack the king of Israel, it was revealed to Elisha by the Holy Spirit, and he in turn told the king of Israel. Therefore, the king of Syria decided to put an end to that.

The amazing thing about that story was the confidence that Elisha had throughout the whole encounter. When his servant told him about the army that had surrounded the city, he replied in today's English, "No sweat or worries. Those with us are more than those that are with them." He asked God to open the young man's eyes, and when his spiritual eyes were open, he saw the mountain full of angels and chariots of fire waiting for orders from Elisha. Now that's confidence, to look at fear eye ball to eyeball and make such a statement. His servant looked in the natural and saw that they were outnumbered, but Elisha looked into the supernatural and saw the provision and protection of God. But it would never have happened if Elisha had not said something, and the reason he had the confidence to know that his God would come through for him, was because he had a history with his God. As the story goes, the man of God asked God to make the creepers go blind (which God did), and He led them straight into Samaria where the king of Israel was. You can start your own history with God today, and it doesn't have to be something big, but I assure you of one thing, it will be big in the eyes of God, because you are starting at your own level. Your angels are waiting for your orders. The scriptures tell us that they increase in strength when they hear the voice of the Word of God (Psalm 103:20), so as your Word level increases, your confidence will increase also, which will eventually increase your testimonies.

That reminds of a story I heard of when I was in Sierra Leone of a minister of the gospel in Nigeria, who was travelling on a highway with his entourage, when they were confronted by highway robbers. The armed men told them to get down from the vehicle, and started demanding money from them. But the man of God simply walked up to the leader, and told them that he pays his tithe to God and not to armed robbers, and went back to his vehicle. He basically defied and dared them to follow the convoy, but the armed robbers couldn't, because the fear of God had fallen on them. Even though these types of testimonies are rare in the Kingdom of God today, it is still available to the Sons of God. If Elisha, who was in the old covenant, believed God and his God came through for him in such a great fashion, how about us that are now in a better covenant? All things are possible to the one that believes his God can do it for him/her (Mk 9:23). The sky is not even the limit to what God can do for His children, but if we keep on believing only for what to eat and wear, when will we move in to the realm of knowing our God, so that we can start doing great exploits for Him (Dan 11:32)? One thing God is passionate about is who will trust Him, so that He can make that person a wonder to the world (2 Chron. 16:9). All throughout His Word, we have seen how He took one man or woman and made them great. That is the reason we see God doing much for one set of people, and not so much for another. We have to take Him at His Word.

THE POWER OF THE MIND

Napoleon Hill, one of the pioneers of the psychology of the power of the mind, had a famous statement, which states, [7]*"Whatever the mind can conceive and believe; it can achieve."* In his famous book, "Think And Grow Rich", which has sold millions of copies, Hill narrated that America is set apart from the rest of the world because here, we are free to believe what we want to believe. That is why success is almost a guarantee to any one that comes to America with a mind to make their dreams happen. What happens is that the mind is free to believe what it wants to, and as such, the possibilities are endless. As a matter of fact, the American dream that a lot of people are chasing after is due to that concept of the limitless nature of the mind. Now if it can happen to people that don't know Jesus, how about the people that have the mind of Christ? There is no doubt that the mind is powerful, but the person with the mind of Christ is capable of achieving what the natural mind cannot even dream of achieving. You don't have to live in fear of gangs. If you can conceive the fact that you are seated with Christ in heavenly places and far above any principality or power, gangs will be like ants under your feet.

That is why we have a responsibility to develop our minds, so that we would be able to think like Jesus thought, and eventually have dominion over the power and influence of the devil. Jesus was never afraid of anything or anyone. He had (for lack of a better word) a child-like trust in His father, that no evil would harm Him until the day that He laid down His life for us. He demonstrated that trust when dealing with the demon possessed, when walking on the water and in storms on the sea, and even to elude His captors when they came to throw Him over the edge of the city (Luke 4:28-30). We can walk in that same anointing too if we develop our minds in Christ, and trust God to protect us from all harm.

Sometimes when we read the Bible, because the stories are thousands of years old and we have heard them over and over, we tend to take them for granted and just look at them as the miracles of the Bible days. But the same God that was in those days is the same God today. He will come through for anyone who trusts in Him. If He did those wonders for the saints in those times, when He was living amongst them in a tent, how about now when the tent has been rent, and He now lives on the inside of every saint? These are amazing times brethren, but we will only do great things if we come to know our God (Dan 11:32). We have a responsibility of developing our mind to the level of the mind of Christ to know fully all of the promises of God, to the point that lack of fear is the normal, instead of the abnormal thing to us.

THE SUPERNATURAL

Friends, this is the realm that the life of Enoch lives in. The Supernatural should not shock and awe us like bombs released over an unsuspecting city. It is our place. God expects that from His children, but most of us are so afraid of that realm that any mention of it is seen as being too "super-spiritual". We are not used in that realm to show off ourselves, but our God. We do not walk in that realm enough, but Jesus said that we will do more than He did. It is His will that we do more than Him. He really means that. He is not in heaven hoping and praying to His father that we don't break His record of the supernatural walk He had while on earth, like an Olympic prodigy protecting his/her record.

When Jesus was walking on the water, He wasn't doing it to impress His disciples; there was no boat left, so He used what He had. The supernatural was natural to Him. Friends we can do greater. Gangs don't stand a chance against our God. I strongly believe that there is coming a time that the Sons of God will be able to walk in the supernatural as easy as breathing air. In these days, the sick will be healed at an alarming rate when we pray, the dead will be raised, and the miraculous will be so natural to us that it will not take days of fasting and prayer to produce results. The power will be readily available, because we will love the presence of our King. Therefore, if a gang member or anyone else threatens a Son of God with a firearm or any type of weapon, it will be so easy to command that person to fall under the power of God, or tell the weapon to become something else, like a banana. I know it sounds like fiction now, but I am looking forward to those days, and I know that it will come, because He has promised that the glory of the latter will be greater than the former (Haggai 2:9). All of that will be done in love, and not just a demonstration of power to show off. It will be to show the enemies of God His power, and cause them to bow down at His feet; seeking repentance.

CHAPTER 4

TOTAL DOMINION OVER (TERRORISM)

THE PHONE CALL

It is September 11, on this beautiful day in the year of our Lord 2001. It is 1520 (3:20 in the afternoon) here in Germany. It has been a very eventful day, and you are about ready to go home in just about over an hour. Your wife called you on your cell phone as a reminder, as both of you had already planned out how you would spend the evening. The only thing in front of you and this relaxing evening is time, so you take it easy and get into your cruise mode for the final stretch of this workday. As a soldier and a Non-commissioned officer in the US Army, you are a leader and duty is no strange word to you, as this has been preached to you time and time again, and you have passed that on to your junior soldiers that you are now in charge of. Even with all of that rich military doctrine, nothing has prepared you so far for the news you are about to receive.

However, for now, you are basking in the thoughts of romance, and the smell of evening dinner prepared by the best chef in the world (your wife), plus the dim lights of romantic candles seems to flirt with your sense of duty. You are exited, because you are a new bachelor, and are still in the process of consummation of the marriage, even though it's been over a month.

Customers love to bring work late, preferably at the last hour of the day, so you resolute in your mind that this is not going to be one of those days. So, you give the order "Hey guys, we are about to enter the last hour of the day, so start rounding up to get to a finish point at about 1630 (4:30 in the afternoon) for clean-up." Your troops are good guys and girls, and they have always done what you have told them to do in your chosen line of work of fixing broken aircrafts in the Army, so there is no doubt in your mind that they will do as they were told by you, and all of you will leave work on time today, even though that is not the norm around here.

At 1600 the phone rings. You wonder who that can be, as it is almost time for clean-up, and missions are known to pop up from nowhere on the last hour of the day. You know that as a soldier, you are on duty 24/7 and whatever the mission is you will execute it without any complaints (at least not in front of your troops), that is, if it is mission related. It is the platoon Sergeant, and he wants all junior (squad) leaders in his office right away.

"What can this be now?", you think aloud to yourself, but you are the man for the job, and so you step out of the office into your boss's office and you find out that everyone is there already, but this time no one is joking around. Everyone is in a serious mood, and that even makes you wonder more what it could be. Without wasting time, the platoon Sergeant closes the door behind him and starts the meeting.

"This is going to be sweet and to the point."

"We have received word from V Corps that there has been an attack on the World Trade Center buildings in New York. Terrorists ran two planes into both towers, and needless to say, there is an unconfirmed amount in the death toll."

"Therefore, we have moved from force protection condition Bravo to Delta. This is all we know for now, so do not say more than you know to your soldiers, as you know this can create fear." "No one is released, and at this time, I need all soldiers to report to the arms rooms to draw their individual weapons and live rounds"

The meeting was quick and to the point, as the platoon Sergeant had said, but as everyone is asking questions, you have one thing on your mind: "How could this have happened?" Needless to say, you know that your evening with the rose of your garden is cancelled, but that is the least of you concerns, as you have now been consumed with this newfound level of duty to serve and protect your country. The man just said force protection "Delta", which means no one is allowed to leave or enter the base. As soon as you inform your soldiers of the news, you make that phone call to your wife to let her know that you may not be coming home that night. The reason she already knows, and there is a sense of understanding between you two that this is more than just a night of not seeing each other to come, as far as this is concerned.

THE UNEVEN DATA EXCHANGE

That was the state of mind of many on September 11, 2008. The word terrorist was used so many times by the media on that day that it caused fear to envelop the airwaves. The terrorists had almost everyone trembling, and some vowed to never fly again. There was an uneven data exchange that took place on that day, and it was the fear of terror for the safety of our nation. However, it is interesting to know that God used the word "terror" in His Word in reference to His people, Genesis 35:5:

"So they journeyed, and the terror of God was upon the cities that were all around them, and they did not pursue the sons of Jacob."

This account was after two of the sons of Jacob (Simeon and Levi) wiped out the whole city of Schechem, after the prince of the city (Schechem) raped their sister Dinah. Reading the whole chapter, we find out that the sons of Jacob tricked the men of the city to believe that they had forgiven the perpetrators, and were at peace with the city. They therefore got the whole city to be circumcised in one day in agreement that if they did that, they would allow their sister to be married to the rapist. When the wound was fresh upon them, they attacked the city, killed every male, and rescued their sister from the house of Schechem. The word of the Lord then came to Jacob to leave the land. He did, and the 'terror' of the Lord came upon the Cannanites so strong that they did not retaliate for the destruction of their city. This was because the fear of the Lord paralyzed them. They couldn't imagine how two men could destroy a whole city, so they said to themselves, "If these two can do that, imagine what all of them combined can do?" To me, this is a pure demonstration of Deuteronomy 32:30, where one can put a thousand to flight, and two; ten thousand. The thousands of men in the city of Canaan could not muster strength to fight, because their confidence was shot by the Lord Himself.

But this is not what is being seen today amongst the people whom Christ died to redeem from the curse of the law (terrorism is a curse of the law). There has definitely been a Data system of exchange in the Church of Jesus Christ. The scriptures let us know that if the foundations are destroyed, there is nothing that the righteous can do, because there will be nothing to build upon (Psalms 11:3). Faith towards God (that He will do the things He promised, such as protecting us from harm) is a basic requirement for the believer (Hebrews 6:1). It is elementary stuff. We do not even need to pray for protection for ourselves, because He has promised us all through His word that He will do that if we do our part. If someone promised to do something for you, do you keep on bothering that individual again and again for the same thing, or take the person's word? In this Data system of exchange that I am talking about, believers don't even realize that the trade was unfair. We take everything coming our way lying down; there is no sign of a desire to fight in us, and so we have become the hunted, instead of the hunter. Many of us are trapped in the prison cells of our minds, because of the fear of trivial issues, such as terrorist attacks. Some of us can't even travel because of the fear of what terrorists will do, but in reality, we are supposed to be the light house of our individual nations, and be the resounding voice of *"this is the word of the Lord in this situation."* If the government sees the confidence of our God in the men and women of God, their confidence is going to rise too.

THAT SPIRIT OF TERROR AGAIN

It is no secret that the world is making the way ready for the anti-Christ. If we look in the world today, we can see that great nations that used to revere the Word of God, and whose forefathers went out of their way to make laws and constitutions which favored the word of God in society, are gradually kicking God out of their governments. In nations like Great Britain and the United States, the freedom and prevalence of the human spirit is called upon, rather than the Holy Spirit who made the human spirit for overcoming every situation of life. This demonic influence that has its bearing from no other place but the pit of hell, forbids the mention of any thing that has to do with the God of the Bible, seeing it as an infringement on their freedom of choice. Like my pastor (Dr. W.J. Moreland) will say, [8]"God is the only One that will bless you to the point that you forget Him." Our nations have forgotten the God who made them great, and so the protection has been lifted away. That is why we are seeing the surge in terrorist activities in our nations.

Please note that I am not after any particular terrorist group, sect, or nation. I am not after the man or woman who causes these attacks, nor am I after the organizations that they represent, because even the world's most hated and wanted man – Osama bin Laden- can be forgiven by our God if he truly repents and accepts the Lord Jesus Christ into his life. I am after the spirit that causes these things to happen. This is plainly evident, as we are now seeing the manifestations of these demonic forces amongst our own kids. We have left off the way of the Lord to raise them, and used every type of therapy and prescription, but have come up short. Instead of love and our physical presence, they have seen us chasing after money (working three or more jobs), while they have been left to solve the riddles of life by themselves. With no one to guide them through it, they have listened to the lies of the evil one, and now they have a personal vendetta against society for the hurt and pain that they have felt all throughout their young lives.

If you read the accounts of the attacks of the Columbine High School of 1999, Virginia Tech campus of 2007, or any such story that you can find, you'll find that their stories are similar; young men and women resorting to terror to bring attention to their pain. It is not new, but an ancient tactic of that devil. So what we are seeing is us winning the war over terror in far away lands, but having it show up right on our doorsteps. That trend can only be from one source that I know – the spirit of terror. The spirit of terrorism has been lying to our kids, and its ultimate mission is to create an atmosphere of fear, so that it can have its way of controlling everyone. That is how satan rules – through fear. The antidote to that spirit is the prayer of faith and the knowledge of who we are in Christ, and not more security forces. The scriptures tell us that we can prepare all we want for the day of battle, but safety in that battle comes from the Lord (Psalm 127:1,2; Proverbs 21:31), and not from our equipment, training, or even our ability to build sophisticated weapons. If we, as believers, grab a hold of this truth, and take it to our God in prayer, our nations in the coalition against terrorism will soon be out of the Middle East.

If you haven't thought about this please think about it for a while. How can a normal person go on a killing rampage to slaughter innocent college mates on a university campus; how can one hack off the hand of another person who does not believe in the god that they serve; how can a militant fighting in a guerilla war take out the live fetus of a pregnant woman, and without any remorse take a smoke break to watch the baby die? I know that the man or woman who does not Know Christ is a son of the devil, (John 8:44) but when we see demonstrations of wickedness to that extent, we have to realize that it is the spirit of terror in operation. It wants to paralyze with its brother, the spirit of fear, and keep us in bondage.

REVERSE PSYCHOLOGY

Knowing all of that," the Enoch lifestyle" refuses to be intimidated by that type, or any type of fear. He/she sees it as an opportunity to show how strong their God is in the lives of those who trust in Him, and present a chance to win over those who have a wrong perception of Him. It sees fear as a reverse psychology that the enemy is using to counter the life of faith, and since it realizes that it has the mind of Christ; it stands steadfast in the Lord. That type of lifestyle calls out fear by its real name, "False Evidences Appearing Real." They know that if they don't back down "fear" will soon tuck its little tail behind its hind parts like a scared puppy does, and run away whimpering. Best of all, it knows that the God of Israel, who has a reputation of never losing a battle, is on its side and that if there is any fear in the equation it should not come from his/her side of the court, but from the opponent's. It is Reverse Psychology, because the enemy is playing with the minds of the believers, knowing full well that this is the only place where it can affect them, and that is only if the believer allows him entrance.

I like the motto of the high performance tires of the Cooper Company tires; [9]"Don't give up a thing." If I could interpret that in Bible language it is "don't back down from fear." It should be the one running, not you. Those who grew up in gangs know exactly what I am talking about. They have mastered this art to perfection, even though they use it for destructive purposes. Having lived a hard life all of their life; if a fight to determine territory breaks out and they are put on the spot, they will not as much as take their eyes from their opponent until he/she backs down. They'd rather fight to the death sometimes, than surrender. That is how we should be like in the area of giving up territory. We are the ones who should be gaining ground, and not giving it up. We have to let this reverse psychology backfire in the devil's face.

All throughout the Word of God, we hear God telling us not to fear. That is because He's got our back, which is another reason why He didn't give us armor for our back in Ephesians 6:13-17. He did not make provision to fall back or fail. We have to have the confidence that our help comes from the Lord, as it says in Psalm 121. It says that our God will not allow our foot to slip, and that He never slumbers nor does He sleep. That means that no matter how bad things may look, if we just trust Him, we will not be harmed. If we can muster that courage in trusting our God, we will start to see His salvation in every area of our lives. When fear becomes a foreign commodity in our lives, then we'll start to see it as something gotten illegally. That is how great men and women of faith whom we read about got to the level that they are. They learned to put their faith in God, use Him as their first and last resource, and come what may; never to give up an inch of territory to fear.

THE ARMY OF THE LORD

When you read this book, "The Enoch Lifestyle," you will be tempted to say that what you are reading is fiction, and that it will never happen. But one thing that I have come to find out about our God is that nothing is impossible with Him, as He thinks big, and not small. It is really up to us what we believe Him for. The Lord is building His army to take over the earth, and there is nothing that any one can do about it to deter His plan. What we are seeing now are only spurts of the glory which is to come to the Kingdom. The church of Jesus Christ is really in its infancy in regards to the knowledge of the full dominion which has been given to it here on earth. The day of the Lord is coming, and it is going to be a terrible time for those that are not in the Kingdom. Please let's get this right; the Lord loves the world and that is why He sent His son Jesus to die for all, but the God of love is also a man of war (Exodus 15:3).

There is coming a time where terrorism, and any such instrument which is used to send fear into the spine of anyone, will be laughed at by the army of this great King. The scriptures tell us all about that in Joel 2:1-11. There is a people coming who will be so strong, of whom the like has not been before their time, nor will there be any like them in the coming generations after them. They are the ones who will establish the full order and glory of the Kingdom of God, whereas their successive generations will sustain it. We are definitely building towards that, but we are not there yet. The scriptures tell us that the fear of them will send a chill in the hearts of the nations.

This mighty army of the Lord will send terror into the hearts of the nations of the world as they do the will of the Lord. Nothing will be able to stop them; the land will be as the Garden of Eden before them, but as a desolate wilderness when they would have passed through. That basically means that their presence will be felt on the earth. In much of today's Christianity, the Church is only known for its spiritualism, and not so much for its economic, social, or political influence. We have a good time in Church, speak in tongues, fall under the power of the Holy Ghost, and enjoy such an emotional high to last us the duration of the church service, but have so little to show for it in the outside world where it really matters. Our transference of the spiritual gifts into the physical to affect our day-to-day life is just too poor at the moment. This will change in those times, as the army will not be as a church on the street corner that no one knows about, but will be a physical demonstration of the Kingdom of God, actively taking over territory, and expanding the King's domain and sphere of influence.

Please note that this great army of the Lord will not be nice as a lot of people consider niceness today (they will not compromise), but will be about Kingdom advancement. They will not be a doormat left abandoned for everyone to step on. Even if the world does not want to recognize them, they will be forced to, because as the world economy fails, this army will shine as the one who gave them the mission. If there are foreclosures and buyouts of large companies, the army of the Lord will be buying out city blocks and bankrupt businesses, to expand the Kingdom of their Father. That is why the world will be pained before them, because the riches of the world will be transferred over to these people. When you touch a man's spending power, you have succeeded in touching his ego.

Literally, no weapon formed against these ones will prosper, because as verse 8 of Joel Chapter 2 states, they will fall upon the sword, but will not be hurt or wounded. Gangs, terrorists, and any weapon of terror that the enemy will dispel against them will not work. They will grasp the full knowledge of the word in Isaiah, "No weapon formed against you will prosper." Because of that, no fear will be present in them, because Jesus Himself will be the head of this mighty army. It is amazing what a man or woman can do without the fear of failure. The reason terrorist groups are so successful is because they have a reckless abandon for the safety of their own lives, and because of that, fear cannot hinder them. Now they can blow themselves up and destroy the physical body and think it's all over, but this army of the Lord will literally be unstoppable, because no physical weapon will be able to break through their defenses.

LIVE IN VICTORY EVERYDAY

Even now I see traces of that mighty army gathering together and waiting for the rest of the army to catch up in the knowledge of the Lord, so that we can bring our Lord quickly to physically lead us and rid this world of evil, once and for all. In the meantime, while we wait, we have to realize that it should be us, and not terrorists or gang members who should scoff at death. If we get this concept, we will soon get rid of any and every type of fear. Have you ever imagined what you can accomplish if there is no fear in your life? We have to not only read the Word of God, but move to the realm of believing it, and from there to the point that we *know* it is true. The Word of God only produces victory and nothing else. We are guaranteed victory all of the time, and not some of the time.

I personally have made up my mind to LIVE (Live In Victory Everyday.) I am not going to live in fear because of terrorists or gangs. I will continue to travel on airplanes and any other means of transportation that the LORD provides; and I refuse to put my family in the inconvenience of moving from safe neighborhood to safe neighborhood. I have read His resume, and if I can give it a number He is 1 million wins to 0 losses. He has never lost a fight. I am convinced and persuaded that I am on the winning team, because I also read the end of the book where I found out that we win both now and at the end. Why should my life be affected and altered by these temporary forces when I have the ancient of days (Jesus Christ) with me? We have to awaken to the knowledge of the One whom we have on the inside of us. Think about this for a moment: Why wasn't Pharaoh able to kill Moses, even though the man hated Moses so much? He was the king of the most powerful nation at that time, and all he needed to do was give the order and Moses' head would be brought to him, right? No, it was not that easy. You see, Moses had the backing of the Lord his God, and that faith was what kept him safe. God had told Him that He would be with him:

So He said, "I will certainly be with you. And this shall be a sign to you that I have sent you: When you have brought the people out of Egypt, you shall serve God on this mountain." (Exodus 3:12)

That faith created a spiritual force over Moses and his brother Aaron, and Pharaoh couldn't touch them. It is one thing for God to speak a Word to us (even audibly), but if we choose not to believe that Word, it will not benefit us. How many of us read the Word of God on a daily basis, but will believe the report on the news media more than those words of life? This is the greatest reason why we don't see a manifestation of God's power in our lives. He has told us in Hebrews 11:6 that without faith it is impossible for us to please Him. He is passionate about someone believing in Him, and that someone can be you today.

Luke 17: 33, says that our lives are saved by our willingness to lose them, and that if any one tries to keep his/her life, that person will lose it. When we fully get the meaning of that, we will gain the attention of the world. We have to come to the point in our faith where we trust in the resolve of our God that we say, "I would rather die trusting in God than live a life of fear at the devil's mercy." That was the place that the three Hebrew boys Shadrach, Meshach, and Abednego got to. In Daniel 3: 16-18, they told the king that their God was able to deliver them from the hand of the king for not bowing down to the king's idol, but even if their God chose not to deliver them, they would still refuse to bow. As the popular story goes, they were thrown into the fiery furnace for refusing to bow down to the king's idol, but the Son of God Himself showed up in the furnace with them, and they were not hurt by the fire. When we believe God to that extent, He will always show up for us every time, and then we will make an impact on our generations, because the glory of God will be there for us.

CHAPTER 5

THE "YOU" FACTOR

The meeting was packed full with business executives. There was barely an empty chair in sight in the 10,000 seat auditorium. Anticipation built up to anxiety; all awaiting the entrance of the business leadership guru. He was the man of the hour. Many had travelled long hours, far and wide, to come and hear what he had to say. When he spoke people listened, because his track record spoke for him; building a fortune 500 company from scratch with no outside help, but total ingenuity and focus; no wonder why he was sought after the way he was.

Finally the wait was over. He made his entrance, and the crowd erupted into a sea of applause. He waved, and with a deep baritone voice replied, "Thank you! Thank you!" The crowd finally quieted down and he said, "Now put your hands together for the most important person in the room besides our God, and that's you." It took some time for the point to sink in, but when they finally got it, they erupted into a long applause for themselves.

This is the state a lot of us Christians find ourselves in today. We celebrate others and really wish them well, but never take the time to consider the fact that we can succeed too. We actually have put success into the hands of the lucky, fortunate, and those in the clique, far beyond the reach of our God, but He cannot do anything for us when our minds are in that state, because just as Proverbs 23:7 states, *"as a man thinks in his heart, so is he."* Take the reality shows on TV for an example. We spend hours watching these shows, and get so passionate about them that we center our schedules around them. We fill our minds with such trivial issues like who the next top model is going to be, or which celebrity is going out with who, or passionately following the story of the next big thing in the world of sports, and by the time we are done, there is no time for the word of God.

That is why when most Christians hold a Bible to read or get in the mood of prayer, they simply fall asleep. They have exhausted the energy needed to do spiritual things, and the reserve 5% can't carry them through in finding what their God has to say about the next day. The sad part about that is that this type of distraction can continue for years, and make anyone miss the plan of God for his/her life. I heard a man of God put it this way: [10]"If all you do everyday is come home from work, take care of the kids, and spend your free time watching some TV until you fall asleep, and that cycle continues faithfully, you'll wake up one day and find out that you are fifty and most of your strength is gone."

Then, all that will be left is a TV set; maybe you'll still have your spouse by your side, and a lot of useless memories that I call junk.

You cannot necessarily use that information for much, except for memories, and that is if you have a good one. The sad part is that in the course of your spending time with that TV set, you actually helped to make someone a millionaire, and a corporation more than stayed in business because of you, as the TV enterprise/entertainment industry turned over millions of the currency of the country that you are in. But you cannot ask them to give you a part of their share, because they used you wisely to get to their destination. What they actually did was use their time wisely. But God is saying to "YOU" today, "My child, use your time wisely. It is your priceless possession. Spend your energy on things that are tangible and that matter; things that have eternal value." Every one starts the day with a level of energy. Then once it is gone, you'll have to recharge your batteries, and that for most people is physical rest, although there is something called waiting on God, which renews our strength. But I am not saying that to leave you clueless. That is something that God put on the inside of you that will work for "YOU."

Also it is not the will of God for you to spend your whole life working for the creditors. Even if you don't believe in being debt-free, common sense tells me that there has to be a time that you pay off that which you owe, so that you don't leave that burden to your children.

Debt is really a burden. Proverbs 13:22, states that a good man ought to leave an inheritance for his grandchildren. That means that there should be enough inheritance to go around to all the children, until it gets to the grandkids. That is why you, my friend, who are reading this book are so important. Two forces in this world have a mapped out plan for your life. Yes, you guessed it right. They are the power of God, and the power of the devil. You may not realize it, but you are who those two forces use to accomplish their purpose on planet earth. Nothing can be done in a vacuum on earth, because earth is a physical world, and the Supernatural world needs man to accomplish its plans. That is why these two forces are after you. You cannot escape it, and you cannot be neutral. There is no such thing on planet earth. Being neutral really means that you've signed up with the power that wants to hurt you. But let's examine these powers and find out which one seeks after your best interests.

SATAN'S PLAN FOR MAN

To understand Satan's plan for mankind, we'll have to go way back before the creation of man. According to Ezekiel 28:12-19, he was created by God and was the anointed cherub that covered. There was no one greater than Lucifer after the Godhead. The scriptures state that he was the model of perfection and beauty; there was nothing more beautiful than him, and he had access to the holy mountain of God where he used to walk on the stones of fire. He was blameless in all he did, giving all the glory to his maker God Almighty, until evil was found in him, and then he was kicked out by the angel Michael and his angels, because he wanted to dethrone the Holy One; that is our God.

"And war broke out in heaven: Michael and his angels fought with the dragon; and the dragon and his angels fought, but they did not prevail, nor was a place found for them anymore in heaven any longer." (Revelation 12:7, 8)

God, in His infinite wisdom and being an omniscient God, knew that Lucifer was going to allow his beauty to fill him with pride and would eventually rebel against Him, so He said in Genesis 1:26, *"Let us make man in our own image and let him have dominion over everything on the earth."* That to me sounded like God put us in charge of a kingdom here on earth. Now the devil wanted a kingdom too, but the difference was that he wanted to exalt his kingdom above the throne of God (Isaiah 14:13), and become more powerful than the Almighty God. I strongly believe that old serpent got jealous that God was spending time with Adam in the Garden of Eden, and wanted to get back at God by having his own kingdom. He was the son of the morning (Isaiah 14:12), and when God created man and started spending time with him (man), he was full of rage and envy, because he was a self-centered creature. That is why Revelation 12:12 states:

"Therefore rejoice, O heavens and you who dwell in them! Woe to the inhabitants of the earth and the sea! For the devil has come

down to you, having great wrath, because he knows that he has a short time."

Like my presbyter will say, (Presbyter Charles A Johnson) *"everyday that dawns and the enemy has not destroyed "YOU" is like a deadline for a late paper."* He knows that the time he has is short, and so he is intensifying his tactics. Make no mistake about it, the devil hated man since the beginning, and nothing can and will ever change that. He knows that he has been condemned to the fires of hell, and so he wants as much company as he can get. Doesn't that remind you of the saying, "Misery loves company"? And yes, the devil is a miserable, pathetic, and frustrated loser, and you don't have to be afraid of him. But hear me well friend, if you are outside the protection of Jesus Christ, and are not born again, you are truly living a danger-ous life, which is like walking on sinking sand. He could kill you at anytime he chooses, but for the grace of God that is preserving you; giving you time to make up your mind for repentance.

THE BELIEVER

Now when someone gets saved and starts to live the God type of life, he/she is protected from the attacks of the enemy, and nothing can harm that person (Proverbs 12:21) However, since God allows everyone to exercise their free will, that person can jump out from under the protection of God through sin, discouragement, and many other weapons that the enemy uses, and open themselves up for destruction. That is why the devil is trying to kill the seed of the Word of God immediately, as it is sown in the heart of the believer (Matthew 13:3-23- parable of the sower). He wants to kill it before it can bear fruit.

However, that old serpent knows that he will never get some saints to go back to the life of sin. He knows that they have been sold out to the Lord, and nothing can pluck them out of the Lord's hand, so he tries to make them as ineffective as possible. Everyone knows that what is ineffective cannot produce its desired result, and so he tries to put things in our path that will distract us from having our fellowship with God. Satan knows that God loves relationships, and since he fell, he has been trying to destroy every relationship that God ordained. He did it in the Garden of Eden, separating Adam and Eve from God, and he is still doing it today in marriage relationships and any relationship that produces unity, because He knows that there is power in unity (Psalms 133). The only unity he approves of is one that will work towards his best interest, and that is why there is great unity in relationships that don't glorify God, at least for a season.

So, he'll try to distract the believer in to doing everything else, but to find out what's written in the Word of God for his or her life. Satan will allow you to go to church regularly and become so engrossed in the work of the church, if he knows that it won't contribute to your spiritual development. What he is trying to do is to cut the believer off from the presence of God, so that times of refreshing won't come from the presence of God (Acts 3:19). As a believer, you need the presence of God on you daily for every situation in your life, and that is what separates us from the rest of the world. The moment you, as a child of God, stop getting refreshed from the presence of God, life starts to get hard. Then, you'll start to make decisions that are not in accordance with God's will.

Please don't think you can run this race on your own strength, trying to make the ends meet through stress, strain, and struggle. You will simply burn yourself out. You need Him in every step of this walk of faith. The Enoch type of lifestyle depends on Him for even the little things in life, knowing fully well that the Lord is his/her source of strength. I strongly believe that it grieves the heart of God to see His children go from job to job trying to look for the right one, or take on too many at a time just to pay a bill, when they could have asked Him for directions and saved themselves a lot of pain and stress. That is affecting a lot of Christian's relationships with their God and their families in developed countries. The effect is a weak prayer life, polarized family members, and unfulfilled promises of God's Word in the life of His saints, which causes frustration. We were never made to supply our own needs. From the beginning, it was not so. Let us not forget that work is good, but sweat (which is actually stress, strain, and struggle) is a curse (Genesis 3:19), and Christ has delivered us from the power of the curse (Galatians 3:13). He wants you to prosper, but He does not want you to labor for riches (Prov23:4). Those are all ways that the enemy tries to make the believer ineffective for the

Kingdom, and if he has a child of God in that position, then he is not afraid of their shouting, running around the church, or even our fellowships. To him, that's all barking and no bite.

GOD'S PLAN FOR US

If you are a parent, or own a pet that looks up to you for sustenance, you must have some form of love that attracts you to either that child or that pet. There is a bond between you and that child or pet that no one understands better than you. Please hear me on this one. That type of love and relationship cannot compare to the longing that God feels for the world to get them in His hands, and protect them from the evil that is coming. However, as much as God loves the world and wants to save everyone, He can't and that is not because He is not able to, but because some people will not allow Him to save them. Outside of Christ, the greatest gift that man has is freedom to make his/her own decisions. He respects our free will, and will not violate it. He is a God that loves relationships, and will do anything to get His children back in His hands. He already did what no one could have ever done, by coming down from His throne to become poor, and die for us. That is how far back God can reach to get man back. So, there is no pain that mankind goes through that God does not feel. He looks upon us in compassion, and wants to help us.

You see, the devil thought it was over for mankind after Adam fell and sin entered the world, but he didn't know that he was dealing with the ancient of days; the One who knew how everything would play out, even before the elements that controlled the world were put into place. You can never out-smart Him and so, when the devil thought that he finally had his own kingdom and that man would be under his control forever, God used His back up plan – Jesus Christ. The devil never expected God to come down from His throne in the form of Jesus the Christ and die for the sins of man, but bless God that He did, and now we can have eternal life in Him if we accept Him into our life. Now the Church, or body of Christ, is seated with Him in heavenly places.

That's why "YOU' are no mistake in the eyes of your God, even if you came as a result of rape. [11]James Robison of Life Outreach International is a perfect example of that. His father raped his mom and she conceived, giving birth to James. However, God had a plan for that young man. It started in 1962 when James started delivering the Gospel of Jesus Christ to the masses through crusades in stadiums and indoor arenas. That led to over two million lives converted to the Lord. Today, he and his wife Betty focus on TV and mission outreach where more people are coming to the Lord in one year than in the first twenty years of their ministry. That is what our God can do if we trust in Him. He fearfully and wonderfully created you. You were in the thoughts of God way before you became flesh and blood. He had mapped out a plan for you before you were conceived in the womb of your mother. This is clearly spelled out for us in Jeremiah 1:5:

"Before I formed you in the womb I knew you; before you were born I sanctified you; I ordained you as a prophet to the nations."

God is a complete God. When He spoke in the beginning saying, *"Let us make man in our own image and likeness"*, He had seen the end state of man from the beginning. He had seen the problems that would come in every generation, and He, in His infinite wisdom, had thought everything through, including the people who would solve those problems. That is why "YOU", reading this book, were not born in the fourteenth century. That was not your era. The people who lived in that time were supposed to solve those problems. Whether they failed Him or not is His to decide, but the good news is that your era is now, and there are things that He wants you to carry out for Him; that is why He brought you out now at this unique time. Believe me when I tell you this: You are not a mistake. You were in the thoughts of Almighty God before the world began. He had a mission lined up for you before the foundations of the world were laid down.

In the beginning, He had you in His mind, and still does; His thoughts are only good for you. The good thing is that if you listen to Him, the least that you will have is a great future and a hope (Jeremiah 29:11). His ultimate goal is the redemption of mankind, and the establishment of His Kingdom. Please don't ignore your time of visitation. You have a fan club that includes the angels, the saints that have gone before you, and the Lord Jesus Christ Himself who are cheering you on. Please make Daddy proud.

WHAT'S THAT IN YOUR HAND

When Moses was about to face Pharaoh in Exodus 4, he was too fearful to go, so after a lot of deliberating with God in order to get out of the assignment, God asked him a simple question, *"What's that in your hand?"* It was a rod that was in his hand. God told him to throw it on the ground, and when he obeyed, it became a wonder to him – a serpent, which eventually became a wonder to Pharaoh and the rest of Egypt. There is something in your hand that will become a wonder to the nations, but the catch is "YOU" have to release it, so that it can work for "YOU." That is why you should not look at the gift He has given to you as something that is insignificant. It is your gift that makes room for you, and brings you before great men or impor-tant people (Proverbs 18:16). Also a man who is diligent in his or her business will stand before important people, or people that will have respect for his/her gift, and not before the tight-fisted and mean folk. In Matthew 25:14-30, the reason the lord was angry with the servant whom he gave the one talent to was not because he did not use the talent, because he said in verse 27 that the servant should have at least given his money (gift) to the exchangers (if he didn't want to use it) and at his coming, he would have been able to generate some interest. It was because the servant despised the gift, and was so ashamed of it to the point that he hid it in the ground.

This lets me know that every child of God is going to be asked to give an account of how profitably they used their gift. That is what the Lord is going to bring; the wealth of the nations to His Kingdom. You are not an insignificant member of the body. Your gift counts in the Body, and the Lord has put that responsibility in your hand to bring His Kingdom here on earth with your gift. Remember also that a chain is only as strong as its weakest link, so until all of us (the body of Christ) are ready, the full glory of the Kingdom will not come. You see, a lot of people are disgruntled in church today, because they faithfully bring their tithes and offerings (if they bring it), and believe God to give them the wealth of the nations, but then go back to that job that they detest, without using what is in their hand. All along, what will prosper them is still in their hands unused. Over the years they become bitter against God, so when God speaks to them to move out in faith for something big, they show forth an indifference that says, "I don't believe that, O mighty God." But God wants to do more for His children.

I believe God is not just interested in giving you a fish when you bring your tithe and offering to Him (which is in the form of a financial breakthrough here and there). We squander that anyway, and come back to Him for more. He wants to teach you how to fish, so you can catch more fish. Anytime you bring an offering to God, you should be listening to the voice of the Spirit for instructions. He will sharpen your spiritual senses, and give you insight for oversight. This is when He sometimes tells you to make a move on an investment, or withdraw that investment. There are many stories of how people withdraw an investment on the stock market, and as soon as they did, the stocks crash. Sometimes, He will lead you into what you need to do to succeed in a business that others have failed in.

Some believers still have a preconceived idea of the revival of the end times; that is very dangerous. They think that the influence that the Church will have in these last days will come as it did in the old days when a whole lot of young people forget about the various works of life. To them, it was earthly and therefore temporal, so they neglected their God-given gifts to focus on winning souls full time, either in full-time ministry on the mission field, or in some other capacity that is related. That right there is why we have this gap between the people who don't know God and the ones that do, which is us. Some few generations ago, Christians saw everything in the world as evil, and so a lot of young men and women neglected good professions, such as lawyers, professors, and politicians, to work in the ministry full-time, regardless of what their inner witness (gift) was saying.

A lot of dreams went unfulfilled, and the grave today is full of potentials that were never reached and dreams that were never realized. We left the office of the attorney, because as people say, "All lawyers are liars"; we left the office of the politician, because again, "All politicians are corrupt." Therefore, now we have the majority of the offices and positions of authority in the hands of people who don't know God, and do we expect them to make laws that favor God's ways? The answer is no. That is why believers don't have a voice in the affairs of the world right now. We are still looking for the days of John Wesley, John Knox, and the Azusa street revival when the Lord has given us gifts to use and to influence the world now, in our time. These individual gifts are the tools that we will use to bring the rest of the world to the saving knowledge of our Savior Jesus Christ. If we continue to shy away from them, we will delay the Lord's coming, because as He said, *"the end will come when this message of the cross is preached all over the world."*

Most times when we talk about greatness, the reason most people don't see their gift as worth anything is because they tend to compare it to other flamboyant ones. But this is a sin in itself, because as I stated earlier, what we are saying to God when we do this is that He gave us something inferior. If my gift is to clean houses or sort out trash, then I should not despise it, because if I do it well, it will eventually bring me before great men. I wonder what would have happened to the ones classified as minority in America and also worldwide if men like Martin Luther King Jr. of the United States and Nelson Mandela of South African had kept quiet. A deliverer would have come by of course, but it may have been another one-hundred years. That is why the "Enoch lifestyle" does not see the gift as inferior, but instead, tries to look for an opportunity to bless God with it. I love to sing and I think I sing well, but that does not move me to try to get a record label, and try to be the next Kirk Franklin or Toby Mac.

Also, as I am an elder in my church, sometimes when my pastor is away I minister to the congregation, but I do not wait in line for my turn to preach, because that may only happen once a year, and I apparently will become disgruntled and leave the place that God has called me to be to receive the Word from His servant. But just as Paul said in Philippians 3:13 *(one thing I do)*, the Lord has called me to write to His body, and I am going to be faithful in that, and make sure that I write every book that He has put in me. It is evident that not all of us are going to be music prodigies and do tours to minister to thousands; neither will all of us have the opportunity to preach every Sunday to hundreds of people. But there is something in each of us that God can use to be a wonder to our generations. There are so many people, both amongst believers and those who don't believe in our God who have used what was available to them, and are now household names in their own world today. These two men are great examples:

EXAMPLE 1- Howard Schultz

Entrepreneur Howard Schultz was one such man. He joined the original Starbucks Company in 1985 when they were selling only coffee beans, and tried to convince them to sell coffee and espresso drinks as well. The idea was quickly rejected, using the excuse that it will distract from the main goal of the company, and that coffee was something to be prepared at home. Therefore, he opened his own company the [12]*Il Giornale* coffee bar chain, and in two years, when the original Starbucks Company ceased making its owners money and was up for sale, he bought it and retained the Starbucks name. Today, the company is the largest coffee making company in the world with over 15,000 stores worldwide in 44 countries. All he wanted was to have a Starbucks on every corner in the United States, and now the company has gone international.

But what did this man see in coffee making that propelled him to the level of a billion dollar industry? He saw something that no man was seeing at that time, and that was value. Schultz noticed that Americans were always on the go, and barely had time to waste, so he cashed in on that and became a billionaire. He didn't go chasing after the steel, oil, or automobile industries that were doing well in those times, nor did he try to beat the up and coming Bill Gates, but stuck with what he knew how to do. There is a scripture, 2 Timothy 1:6, that most of us who believe the way of the cross read and miss altogether. It says:

"Therefore I remind you to stir up the gift of God which is in you through the laying on of my hands."

We think that Paul was talking of only spiritual gifts and nothing else. But that is not so. I believe that the laying on of the hands brought alive the spiritual, as well as other gifts that were in the young man Timothy. Stirring also means to add value. He was telling Timothy to add value to what was within him, and that is why in the next

95

verse, he charged him that God had not given him a Spirit of fear, but of power, love, and a sound mind. Fear can cripple your gift, making you feel inferior to everyone else. So please add value to your gift and maximize your potential. The Enoch type of life is not intimidated by other gifts, but will work its own with diligence, so that it will produce fruit in time.

EXAMPLE 2 - Peter J. Daniels

Maybe you are the type of person who loves to talk and always loves to encourage people, but you think you lack the necessary education to do that professionally, or to become a motivational speaker. Then allow the story of [13]Peter J. Daniels to encourage you, and spur you on. He came from a very disadvantaged background. Nobody from his family had made any impact on society, as he said in over five-hundred years, and by the way his life was going, he was certainly heading down the same path. Many of his relatives had been to jail at least once. At the age of twenty-six, he was still an illiterate, because he started school so late, being that he was battling with the disease diphtheria. He failed in every grade in school. He therefore became a bricklayer; a stonemason.

But something happened on May 25 of 1959 when he was twenty-six years old that changed his life for good. He went to a Billy Graham crusade and got saved. At that time, he was hopelessly in debt, so he started reading biographies of successful people, and made it a personal adventure to educate himself in fields like science, history, business, and anything that could contribute to his personal development. After reading over six thousand biographies, he launched out into business. He lost all his money, and went bankrupt not once, but three consecutive times. But he didn't give up on the vision that was burning in his heart and get himself a good 9 – 5 JOB (which he calls 'just over broke'), even though his wife wanted him to. He chose vision and purpose over security, and followed the dream that God placed on the inside of him. He eventually succeeded in establishing one of the most lucrative real estate empires in Australia with connections in South East Asia. Now, instead of taking care of only his family, his focus is helping believers worldwide.

Today, he is a voice sought after in the business world by not only large business corporations, but also by leaders of nations. He has served on international boards covering the face of the earth, and realizes that his influence has given him a worldwide audience who listens when he speaks. Corporations have been known to pay him up to a million dollars for a fifteen-minute session of advice. He has a no-debt philosophy of approach in business, and as you can tell, he got that from the Bible. His latest goal is to get as many Christians in English-speaking countries in business through the local church, so as to generate $200 billion dollars for world evangelism in the next twenty years. If you ask me, I'll tell you that this man is leading the Enoch type of life.

Friends, there is no excuse not to use what God has given to you. That gift that you despise can take you places you have not even imagined in your wildest dreams if you stir it up – place value on it, and maximize it. If Peter Daniels can do that as a child of God, you can too. It proves that all men are born equal before God, but it is the value that you place on your gift that separates you from the crowd. I realize that not everyone will own large corporations like Peter J Daniels. If that happens, then who will be the hands in the Kingdom to carry out the vision? However, my point is this. If God has placed a vision in you, He is more than able to bring it to pass. Maybe yours is to rise up in the ranks to a place of authority and influence in your place of work, and has nothing to do with ownership. Whatever it is, don't be mediocre about it; follow the voice of the Spirit, and He will definitely lead you into every truth. You see, if you are willing and obedient to follow diligently the purpose of God for your life, your praises, instead of some atheist's, will be sung tomorrow. Just as I used Peter J. Daniels and Howard Schultz, so your story will be told. What you are going through right now is a potential testimony that will help someone tomorrow, if you allow God to finish the work.

PREPARATION

What am I saying here? Am I suggesting that all of us who have the traditional 9-5 jobs should abandon them and follow our dreams blindfolded? Of course not; however, one thing is certain, God has put a lot of us in these jobs for preparation for what He has for us tomorrow. For some of us, those jobs are our promised land. For some others, they are not. Have you ever wondered why it took eighty years for God to talk to Moses in the burning bush, and send him to go and deliver His people, or why David did not immediately become king of Israel after he was anointed by Jesse in 1 Samuel 16? It was all because of preparation. Those men and many others in the Bible whom God tasked to do His will, had to get ready for the work of the Lord. We are no different. Even our Lord Jesus Christ had to go through a time of preparation. At twelve, he made His first appearance in ministry in front of the scribes, Pharisees, and Sadducees (Luke 24:1-52), but it took Him another eighteen years to enter in to full-time ministry. He had to grow in wisdom and stature (verse 52). He grew in wisdom; that's why He always outwitted His accusers, and He grew in stature; that's why He had the stamina to drive. There is a time of preparation for the ministry that God is calling us to. It really does not take God any time to do a work, as He is the Alpha and Omega (beginning and the ending), but He has to develop the vessels (us) whom He is going to use to do the work. That development is what takes time, and for some saints it takes longer than others, as God has to break, mold, and shape them based on their level of obedience.

However, God knows when we are ready, because in his infinite wisdom, He alone can tell when we are or not. There is a level of obedience He is looking for that we have to get to, in order for Him to trust us with the true riches of His Kingdom. That is why when those temptations and trials come our way, we should count it all joy. We are being tried and proven for what is before us, but if we keep failing the tests, we prove to Him that we are not ready. If He allowed His Son to be tested in the wilderness by the devil, knowing full well that His eternal plan for mankind would be foiled had Jesus failed; we should see ourselves as no different when it comes to temptations. I must say this to you child of God, just as He had faith that His Son will not fail Him, so does He have faith that you will not fail Him, but will get it right today (God deals in the present). That is why He has not taken His gifts away from you, even though you have fallen down so many times.

Therefore, I am not asking you to quit your job now, and allow your family to suffer if you just have ambition, but no direction by the Holy Spirit. That is why we need to develop a real relationship with Him, so that we can hear when He speaks. However, if you are not using laziness as an excuse, but absolutely dislike what you are doing to bring the money in to take care of your family, you may be in the wrong field. My pastor would ask it this way, "If you are given $2 million right now, will you still do what you are doing?" If your answer is no, then you need to start an exit strategy today, and depending on you, it might take a year, or twenty years to exit that job, and get into what you love doing. If it's not your passion, why stay in that job and live a miserable life? There is good news and light at the end of the tunnel, because we can really shorten the time by the way we prepare. The men and women of the Bible didn't have the cloud of witnesses that we have now, but we do through the Word of God, biographies of others in recent history that have succeeded in the area we want to embark upon, and the greatest of all, the leading of the Holy Ghost. He is our helper, and He knows the way. Let's trust Him.

CHAPTER 6

HE WANTS A KINGDOM

The Kingdom of God/Heaven is a very wide subject, so I don't intend to spend a lot of time on it, but my intent is to give a quick synopsis on the Kingdom, as it relates to "The Enoch Lifestyle." There are very good books on this topic that I recommend everyone to read. One such is [14]Dr. Myles Monroe's, "Rediscovering the Kingdom." God loves the church, but let me be quick to point out that what He is seeking is a Kingdom, which means the King's domain. He is the King, but He has charged us with the responsibility of bringing His domain here on earth. He wants it to be established here on earth, because as Matthew 6:10 states, His Kingdom is already established in heaven. Notice that I didn't say church, but the Kingdom. We believers have relegated the word "Church" to the level of the gutters; to the extent that when it is mentioned, people have negative feelings of poverty, sickness, and lack of power, but from the beginning it was not so. In 1Timothy 3:15, the Lord calls His church the pillar and foundation of the truth. Don't get it confused with a building with four or more walls. But if one can ask, why is the Church of Jesus Christ so lifeless?

HEADLESS

The reason is because it is headless; we are detached from our source, and any living thing with its head cut off will struggle and eventually die. We have succeeded in dethroning our King all by ourselves, and have had the audacity to dictate the terms and conditions of His rule in His own Kingdom. He is a Mighty King, and as we all know kings are not dictated to; instead, they do the dictating. There is no kingdom that disregards their king like the Kingdom of God. In every other kingdom, like the ones we have known here on earth, such disobedience calls for the head of the offender. In other words, the king says, "Since you don't respect the head of this kingdom, I will have your head." But our King is not like that. He is the most patient King that I know, and yet we disrespect Him by having our own agendas and wills on top of His, which He has explicitly given to us in His Word. His Holy Spirit sometimes has to plead with us for days that, in some instances, turn into years in trivial issues like unforgiveness though it looks likes nothing, slows downs the operation of the Kingdom and the prosperity of the Kingdom.

At other times, we disrespect Him by the unbelief that we display towards Him. I'm talking of what He has already said in His Word. If He has already promised us the nations, will it be a problem for Him in granting us the little things in life that we lust after so much? We have to realize that it is not about us, but about His Kingdom. He decides what He wants in His Kingdom and how much power, influence, and wealth that it will have. We just have to follow Him. That is why when the Holy Spirit speaks to an individual in the Kingdom to make a move that will bring about wealth, and that person disobeys thinking it is too extravagant, that individual is being disrespectful to the King, and is also robbing the Kingdom of its advancement.

Let's say God told you to believe Him for a hotel chain – I mean to own hotels. Then, you disobey thinking that such a thing cannot necessarily happen to a person like you with so little education. What you have done is rob a saint who may have needed a job like that to care for his/her family. Also, you may have robbed another by allowing the thought that, "wealth is only found in the hands of the people who don't know God", and let that thought gain a stronghold in that person's heart. I am talking of the idea most people have that say you have to be evil to be wealthy, because money is evil, and the righteous can't have it, since they are so meek and forgiving; they cannot cross people the wrong way to have their pot of gold. That of course is wrong, as the Bible states clearly in 1 Tim 6:10, that it is the *"love of money"*, not money, that is the root of all evil. We really need our Head who is Christ, the Head of all the Church to understand all that He has in store for us – Eph 4:15.

HE WANTS TO EXPAND HIS KINGDOM

The man or woman with the Enoch type of faith is one who seeks to expand the Kingdom of God, instead of his/her own church activities. You see, satan stole the inheritance from man (that is this earth) when Adam sold his birthright by falling into sin (Genesis 3). When that happened, mortal man lost the legal right to this world, so the devil became the god of this world (2 Corinthians 4:4). That is why what Jesus did, by dying on the cross for our sins and rising up from the dead, is the best thing that ever happened to mankind, since the fall of man. He redeemed us from the curse of the law, and so now we are free to exercise dominion here on the earth like God intended from the beginning. Even though God created the world, He cannot legally do anything in the world. He wants a body, and since He is Spirit and dwells in heaven that is why He wants YOU to dominate the elements of the earth, just like He said it in the beginning. We have to give Him the legal right to operate in this world. This is why He wants to, and will, give us the world, and then turn around and destroy it; to give us a new one as mentioned in Revelation (don't cry about it; it is defiled anyway).

The first mention of the Kingdom in the New Testament was by the man whom God sent to precede Jesus, John the Baptist, and what he proclaimed was not some denominational organization, because they had enough of that in the form of the Pharisees, Sadducees, and teachers of the law. He proclaimed the Kingdom; warning men to prepare the way for the King. Even Jesus Himself started His ministry by proclaiming that *"the Kingdom of Heaven was at hand (near us)"* Matthew 4:17. He never once mentioned anything about a building (except, when He spoke about the destruction of the temple or His body), but in his daily teachings the people heard Him talk about the Kingdom of God all throughout His ministry. That is why the scribes and teachers of the law never understood His message, because they blocked the way of everyone who was seeking to enter into the Kingdom of God, while at the same time refusing to enter for themselves. They wanted the Kingdom to be restricted to those of the Jewish descent, so that the Jewish religion and the temple could be preserved, but He had the whole world in mind. You see, every King seeks to expand His Kingdom, so He wasn't tolerating their little vision of me, myself, and I. A lot of us in democratic societies have a problem with this type of mentality, but the Kingdom is not about a democracy. It is about a theocracy; where God is the King, and all orders come from Him, and no one else.

When they asked Jesus about the time-frame of the appearing of the Kingdom of God, He told them that the Kingdom of God was not going to come with a special celebration of recognition. Neither will one say it is here or there, but that the Kingdom of God was within them. This also lets me know that if the Kingdom of God is in us, we have the responsibility of bringing it out to the world, and that process takes time, but as the knowledge of God increases in the earth, so will the Kingdom expand. They were in religion, but the Lord was about His Father's business. Myles Monroe put it this way, *"religion is about denominations, but the Kingdom is about communities."* The Lord wants to build a strong community with you in mind, and it is coming to your area, so please be ready.

KINGDOM MINDSET

You see, if we get this Kingdom mindset, we will not retaliate when we are wronged, or try to use this world's system to get revenge when someone offends us. Our Kingdom is not of this world, so the system of operation is quite different from that of the world we are living in. In our Kingdom, there is no separation of Church and State. The sole purpose of the Church is to establish the State, which is another word for the Kingdom. There is nothing democratic about our Kingdom, because the word of the King is final. We do not have to vote for an agreement, because the government is purely theocratic; Our God is in charge, and no one else. His Word is pure, and any other type of word would not stand the test of time. If we really get this Kingdom mindset, the world will be purged from all evil, because we will bring the Kingdom of God here on earth, and even though there will be opposition, nothing can stand in our way. The world that we live in is bleeding from the effects of sin, and until the bleeding stops; the wound cannot be treated. When administering first-aid to any bleeding victim, the first thing that the first-aid worker tries to do is to stop the bleeding. Without the clotting of blood to stop the blood flow, the plexus of vessels may even dilate to allow the blood to flow more freely, and this is what normally leads to death.

The treatment that world leaders have been giving the world is as such. We have been trying to heal the wound without stopping the bleeding, and anytime that happens we open the arteries more and more, to the point that the earth is gradually dying on us. Instead of man stopping the sin (which he cannot because it is his nature), he finds every other way to pass the blame, and looks for temporary solutions for a permanent problem in every other place, except in God. That is why the present earth will pass away, and God will bring about a new one (Rev 21:1), because it is going to bleed to death. Since the tower of Babel (Gen 11:1-9), mankind has been trying to fix this problem without any help from God. What has that caused us; wars and natural disasters, such as earthquakes, storms, and famine? A lot of people will argue that these things have always been with man, but look at the intensity and frequency of these occurrences today, and you'll see that they are on the rise. A great example is the 20th century, which was the deadliest century to date; [15]WWII alone claimed well over sixty-million lives.

The world is blind to these things, because the god of this world has blinded their minds to that truth (2 Corinthians 4:4), but we have to show them by bringing our Father's Kingdom here on earth. Our Kingdom is really not of this world, so we don't have to adopt this world's way of doing things. When the children of Israel tried to adopt that system in 1 Samuel 8, God, through the prophet Samuel, told them of the repercussions, but they refused to listen. Therefore, God gave them a king, and that started their woes. In verse 7 of that chapter, God told Samuel that it wasn't Samuel the people didn't want anymore, but Him (God). That right there is proof that any nation which breaks away from following after the God of Israel will surely fall like Israel eventually fell to Babylon and the Romans, regardless of how long it takes. This is why every system of government in the past, including the democratic ones, failed and will continue to fail, because those systems of government, like the people of Babel, all wanted a kingdom, void of the influence of God. They wanted to be like God without God's help, and that is impossible. Mankind cannot even start to fix the world's problems with our limited minds, even with all our knowledge and technological advancement.

If we have this Kingdom mindset, we will pray for people who intentionally hurt us, as Jesus did on the cross, and not try to get even. Why; because of the resolve of our King. He says it is a fearful thing for anyone to fall into the hands of the living God (Heb 10:31). Knowing this, why do we take matters in our own hands sometimes? It is because we don't trust that He'll come through for us. In my walk with God, I have personally seen God deal with people who despised, talked bad about, and were even planning evil against me, to the point that I prayed for mercy for them. A lot of people will say that is coincidence, but I know it wasn't, because it has happened to me every time someone came against me, and I turned them over to the Lord without malice (I don't want to go into detail, because I love these people and have forgiven them).

If we learn these principles of the Kingdom, and start applying them, we will see a lot of our "so-called" enemies be converted to the Lord, without even preaching to them. If we would allow God to fight our battles, instead of filing a lawsuit, we would see the hand of God at work, and the eventual salvation of that person who hates us. If perhaps you disagree with me, ask yourself this question, "Are you interested in seeing that person fall down at the foot of the cross in repentance, or your ego satisfied by you winning the case?"

God is not interested in just punishing people and sending them to hell. He wants them to come to know Him too, and become converted into His Kingdom; therefore, He'll sometimes allow the person who does not know Him to go through some discomfort, so that they can call on Him for help. God is a God of love, and we have to realize that even in those times that He takes lives it is for the eternal good, so that particular incident will cause more people to repent and turn to Him. Sometimes that person is a stumbling block to God's Kingdom, and He, in His infinite wisdom, has seen the end from the beginning; knowing that this person will not come to His Kingdom, but will instead prevent its expansion. Examples are the story of the killing of the first born in Egypt (Exodus 12:29-33), and the slaying of Herod (Acts 12:21-24). He has mapped out a plan for the establishment of His Kingdom, and anything or anyone that tries to hinder it will be taken out. The establishment of the Kingdom is very important to our God.

A UNITED CHURCH

I want to really re-emphasize the point that His Kingdom is a theocracy, and not a democracy. The minister of the Gospel who is walking in the Enoch type of lifestyle realizes this, and will refuse to be voted into office. He realizes that if man voted him or her in office; man can vote him/her out, but when God chooses, He does not change His mind. His Kingdom is not divided or classified into racial and ethnical backgrounds. That is why the terms black church, African church, Hispanic church, or any other division is not acceptable in the language of the Kingdom. There is no place for it period, because the body of Christ is not divided, but one. When the Lord comes back, He is not coming for a Hispanic, black, or Pilipino Church; He is coming for His church; and that is the unified Body.

If the Lord has His Kingdom in mind, shouldn't we also? But that's not what we have in the Body of Christ today. We are a group of individuals who just want to feel good for the moment in church, and after we get out of there; go right back into our works of flesh. We hear the Word of God, but it seems to have no effect on a whole majority of us. That is because we use the Church as a means of a spiritual high like a junky on crack cocaine. After the high is gone, depression sets in. We harbor hate, malice, jealousy, unforgiveness, and every type of devilish work in our hearts, and we wonder why we don't prosper. We put on this Christian, churchy mask in the parking lot, right when we are about to step out of our cars, and press the pause button on our disagreements just to put up this act of love, then, pick it up right after church. That's why there is no power in the Body. I used to wonder why the blessings of God, which He promised in the scriptures, are not manifesting in the Body of Christ, but I don't anymore. Now I know that we are not ready for them. If God releases them; we will kill ourselves, like a kid in a candy store. The Church has really become like a powerful sports car (let's say a 626 hp Mercedes Benz-Mclaren) in a garage that is continuously broken. It brings no honor to its maker, as king of the road, by being in the shop all of the time. That is what we have become. At a time when a lot of us should be harvesting souls and ministering to the saints, we cannot, because we ourselves need fixing too.

AN EXAMPLE FOR OUR TEENS

But "YOU", reading this book, are the Lord's battle-axe. You are whom He will use to show the nations His awesome power and might. YOU have been charged with that great honor of bringing the glory of God to the unbelieving. It is only by you that they will come to know our God, and have a desire to be part of His Kingdom. Please pause and think about this off the wall question for a minute: What is the greatest challenge that we have with many of our Christian teens? Just in case you didn't have the answer in the allocated three seconds, please let me help you out. It is the problem of identity. They want to identify with the rich, famous, and the "so-called" successful of this world, which ride in nice cars and wear fancy clothes. In their own lingo, "That's what Cool". That is why, in our culture today, fashion is really in the hands of the young people. They are the one's being highly targeted more than any other age group by designers and advertisers, because they are the ones who are always concerned about the new "this" or "that".

Ask the young people about the latest outfit, celebrity, or music star and they will tell you with little mental strain, but ask them about influential Christian people in the world, and then the mental strain sets in. The problem is that even though there are some of us who are making strides in the financial, social, and economic world, the numbers are too significantly small for world recognition. When believers are mentioned, what comes to mind is only the spiritual, and nothing about the physical. People think that we are so out of touch with anything physical, that they don't bother ask our opinion for anything. It is not that some people don't want to identify with the body of Christ, but we have done a poor job in giving them a reason to come over to the Lord's side. Please don't get me wrong on this one. If anyone is ashamed of the Gospel, the Lord will be ashamed of him/her before His Father, and that goes for our teenagers too, but I really believe that we have a responsibility to show the glory of the whole Kingdom, so that we do not cause someone to stumble. Isaiah 2:1-4 should be our focus. When the people who don't believe in our God see what He is doing in our lives, they will come running to Zion asking us to teach them how to make it out there in that cruel world.

Some of us will not push to accomplish our purpose in life, but will hope for our children to bail us out when they grow older, especially if they have a lucrative talent, like in sports or music. This is not representing the Kingdom the right way, as the scriptures let us know that we should leave an inheritance for our grand-children, not only our children (Proverbs 13:22), and not the other way around. That is why a lot of us have to struggle in life, because our fathers and grand-fathers did not leave any inheritance for us, and we have to begin from the starting point. We never had a jumpstart in life. Now I am not putting blame on the parents who don't know this Word; however, if you are in the Kingdom of God and know this Word, there is no excuse for you not to work your gift and leave an inheritance for your children's children.

Today is not too late to start. We should not be cheering junior on, while sitting back waiting for him to bring a payback years from now. When they see our diligence, they will be motivated to do the same, and so continue the tradition of wealth in our families. That is why when you hear of some family names, you can attribute wealth to the members of that family. I don't need to mention any name here. We all know those affluent families in our societies.

That is why, as I said earlier, we should not shy away from the riches that the Lord is about to bring to the Kingdom. We should be able to prosper, not only financially, but also in every area of our lives. They are our God-given possessions, but if we don't possess them, they will continue to be in the hands of the god of this world. He gives them freely to his children, and they, in turn, use it to promote the kingdom of darkness. The person who is not Kingdom minded sees it as a waste to give a penny towards the furtherance of the Kingdom of God. They will simply tell you, "I'm not giving my money to that church, so that the pastor can buy more fancy clothes and nice cars." They will instead waste thousands of the world's top currencies on wild parties and social gatherings that will bring pleasure to them, and their close friends. When they want to feel close to God, they will give millions to charities that have nothing to do with the Kingdom, because they want the recognition and the feeling that by helping the poor, they will gain entrance into God's heaven. We know the answer to that.

We who know the Truth about the Kingdom don't have the kind of money to support our Father's work, and yet we are fighting to stay poor and humble. It is indeed a twisted and perverted conception of the word "humility", and I don't mean the humility part. We prefer to have a church fund that runs from our generation to our children's children, instead of inheriting our Father's wealth, and do the thing the Kingdom way. We don't want to search after the Spirit of wisdom, and wait at the posts of His doors (Proverbs 8:1-4), so that we can have an epiphany on the situations of life. Let's pause for a moment and think about this: What is really stopping the advancement of the Kingdom of God and His children in the physical world? Let me help you out again. It is money. So why do we fight against having it? Many people will say because money is the root of all evil, but as we know that is not correct, as we saw earlier in this chapter. The Enoch type of faith learns to divide the Word of God correctly, so that he/she does not consume what is not edible to their Spirit.

The correct reading of that scripture in 1Timothy 6:10 is:

"The love of money is the root of all kinds of evil, for which some have strayed from the faith in their greediness, and pierced themselves through with many sorrows."

If you love God and not money, then you will seek the further-ance of His Kingdom. The problem starts when "church folk", not Kingdom-minded folk, love money more than God. That is when we start to see every type of back-stabbing and work of the flesh, but if we seek after the Spirit of wisdom and not money, enduring riches will find their way into our lives (Proverbs 8:16-17). There is a vast difference between the church-minded folk and the Kingdom-minded one. The "church folk" seek to promote the church agenda, and will do everything, including closing the door to the Kingdom of God, while refusing to enter themselves, as long as the church curriculum is in tact.

CHAPTER 7

A PASSION FOR HIS PRESENCE

WHAT IS PASSION?

It was on the first Saturday in July of 2008. My wife and I were on our way to intercessory prayer in Kitzingen, Germany. I was driving a Volkswagen Passat on the autobahn, and was doing about 140 Km/hr, which is about 90 Miles/hr. I thought I was the king of the road, because at that time, everyone was giving way to me, as I was coming through on the left lane. Then, from nowhere, I saw a pair of lights behind me; they seemed to be about 5 miles down the road, and so I thought I had time before the car catches up with me. I continued on the same side of the road, and in what seemed like a couple of seconds, the sports car (VW Touareg) was right behind me flashing lights for me to get out of the way. I sped up to 100m/hr or about 160km/hr, but the driver had no trouble keeping up. I said to myself, "Oh you're in for it now. I am going to bury this needle." I then went on to 120m/hr, but the driver showed no sign of slowing down, so I moved out of the way. We gave way to that sports car, and she sped down the road as if we were standing still, doing probably 160m/hr, approximately 260 km/hr with ease.

That really is very common in a country like Germany where on many stretches of the autobahn there is no speed limit. Basically, you can go as fast as your vehicle can take you, but on that day it hit me. "That is my example of a person with passion", I said. That driver had a passion to pass, and no matter what, even if she had to go around us, she demonstrated that she was going to pass us one way or the other. That type of passion this lady demonstrated puts me in remembrance of Psalm 42:1:

"As the deer pants for the water brooks, so pants my soul for You, O God."

It is the type of following after, which refuses to give up until that desired thing is met, whether it is a physical need or refreshing from the presence from the Lord. But what is this thing called passion? Let's look at the dictionary definition of that word. There are many definitions for the word passion in the dictionary; however, I like this one from dictionary.com better. *Passion*: *any powerful or compelling emotion or feeling, as love or hate.* It is the fire in any relationship that keeps the relationship flames ablaze, and even though some people may not consider it necessary, it is very essential in a love relationship, because the day the passion in any relationship dies; the love starts to die too. Passion is what will make a man brave through a storm just to see the love of his life. It is what gives a woman extra strength to prepare her husband's favorite meal, even after a stressful day at work.

It is the motor in any relationship, and if I can call it another name, I would say chemistry.

Before you read any further, may I just ask you how your chemistry is between you and your God? Are you still chasing after Him like the time you first found Him, or rather the time He first got your attention? Are you still seeking after Him in the nighttime when everyone is asleep, and spending time in His Word to try and understand His ways, or has someone or something else stolen your attention, and now you have taken your gaze from Him? If the answer to those questions is no, there is still time to get your passion back, and learn to love Him all over again.

Any man or woman who has ever been deeply in love and fallen out of it knows what I am talking about. In the beginning of the relationship you could hardly keep those two apart. They were always together and (for those that love to cuddle) you could not put a knife in between the two, as they were always in each other's arms. They could not find any fault in each other, and even if there was it was easily overlooked as a minor offence. But in many cases in marriage relationships one may ask; "What caused the switch that each person is now at each other's throat, until both end up in court fighting over the kids and the material things, to find out who had a right to what? The answer is simple. The passion in either one, or both of those lovers, has died and unless it is revived again, that relationship is headed for the rocks.

The old folks knew a thing or two about this word passion. The chemistry between them and their God was right. They did not necessarily have the knowledge that we have today, but they loved God with all of their heart. Those were the mothers and fathers who had an activity everyday in church to stay occupied in the Lord's vineyard. That was definitely an extreme, because they didn't have time to impact their communities effectively as they should have, as they spent all of their time in church, and had time for nothing else. I can talk about that, because I grew up in one of those churches, and mine was a Pentecostal one that would spend all day in church on Sunday. The interesting thing that I noticed over the years in my years in church is that as those churches took a backseat to the charismatic movement, the passion that was in the churches decreased, instead of increased. Now we meet for meetings two, or the most three times a week, and the knowledge coming over the pulpit is so full of insight and revelation that the congregation of our present churches can even teach the pastors of those years. We now have Bible on CD, on the web, on i-pods and there is no shortage of cross-reference materials for the study of God's Word. But what has really happened to the passion that was once in the church, in especially industrialized nations?

THE PRESENTATION

Surprisingly, as I have noticed in the body of Christ, the answer to part of that question is our presentation of the Gospel. Too many ministers of the Gospel present the Word of God as an option for the victory that the Bible tells us we are entitled to in this present life and the life to come. We are too optional, and as such there is no real hunger for the things of God. We come to God with a Burger King restaurant mentality (Have it your way) with one thing in mind, which is: *"If you don't treat me right, I'll take my money and find another that will give me the same, or maybe even better service down the road."* Therefore, that attitude trickles down to the people, and so we have a whole generation who think they are doing God a service by just showing up once a week to check the block that they were in church that week. There is really no pursuit for the deep things of God, and if there are some who dare to pursue, they think that they've been called into the five-fold ministry. That is why you can ask most saints on a Monday or Tuesday night if they'll be attending the midweek Bible impact or midweek service, and they may have to go into a time of fasting and prayer for an answer. But as my pastor (W. J. Moreland) will always say, *"When we were sinners, we planned out our sinning days meticulously."*

For those of us who loved the club, it would be crazy for someone to ask us even on a Monday if we will be going to the club on Saturday of that week, which is five days away. But why do we treat God that way and expect the best from Him? This, I believe, is why we are not seeing the move of God in western nations. God is not partial. He has promised to give us everything if we ask Him, and that includes revival. If you follow this God passionately, He will give you what you are seeking liberally.

But this is the same Gospel of the Kingdom that men lost their lives for, while we are taking it so lightly. Some men and women were beheaded, some were stoned to death, others were crucified upside down, and yet others thrown into dungeons for wild beasts to devour; yet they didn't give up. The only reason that we can read and translate the sixty-six books that God chose to give to us as His word is because those patriarchs had a love and a passion for the Lord, and wanted to see His Kingdom established on earth, as it is in heaven. David rightly called that *the zeal for the house of the Lord* in Psalm 69:9. He said that the zeal for the house of God had eaten him up.

I can fully understand what the Psalmist David was saying in that scripture. He was talking about passion for the presence of God. This is the level that you get to in God where nothing else matters but pleasing Him, and so your single-minded devotion for His presence propels you to get to the place where billows of his love go freely over you; bringing times of refreshing from the presence of the Lord. That was the place David was talking about when he said in Psalm 42:7 *"Deep calls unto deep at the noise of your waterfalls; all your waves and billows have gone over me,"* and also in Psalm 89:15, which says, *"blessed are the people that know the joyful sound..."* In that place, the sound of the Spirit is not hard to hear and respond to, and that is the place that Enoch got in God, and where we can all get to as well.

SINGLE-MINDEDNESS

If we are honest, we can see that single-mindedness in people who don't even know the God we serve. Muslim extremists who give their lives as suicide bombers for a cause that is perishable are prime examples. For a man or a woman to defend their faith or cause to the point of death, you know that they must be serious about what they believe in. In today's evangelical circle, I am sure that not even 50% of us have that type of devotion to the faith that we practice. I am not trying to say that we have to go back to the days of the first apostles, because if there is anyone more grateful that they were not born in those ages it is I. I appreciate the fact and thank God for it that I can openly carry a Bible without being taken to the gallows for execution. However, what I am pointing out here is that until we have the same devotion for the things of God that the apostles in the Bible had, we cannot make much of an impact on this world.

The extremists who become terrorists had the message of Islam presented to them as the only way, and that their personal plans and goals were always secondary to the cause that they believed in, and that started since they were babies feeding on milk. Over the years, they grow up with that single-mindedness that you cannot convince them otherwise, except by the intervention of the Holy Ghost. There-fore, when they are called upon to give their lives for the cause as a suicide bomber, it is not a surprise, but to them; an honor. That is why if their plans to carry out a suicide mission go awry, and they are caught they will desire the death penalty, instead of a life sentence, so that they can be martyred. To them that is failing the 'cause.' It is a great dishonor to them.

CONFORMITY TO THE WORLD'S SYSTEM

The other reason why there is not so much passion amongst us is because of the options which are available to us through the world's system. In today's world, if you need money right now for anything, whether it is a necessity or not and have good credit, your chances of securing that money through the banks will greatly increase. If you, your family member, or loved one is sick and you have the money for the surgery or whatever medical attention that is needed, the chances of the illness claiming the life of that individual will be slim to none. If you get into any legal trouble, and you have the money to secure a very good lawyer, (one that has a good reputation of winning cases), then the chances of going to jail will again be slim to none, especially if you are innocent. All of the above named solutions are not evil, and sometimes they are the ways that God wants to use to deliver us out of the troubles that come our way, but the problem is when we start to rely and put our faith in that system. Any time our faith is in a system other than the one God has prescribed for us, we are in trouble.

Jacob was a trickster, and it was through trickery that he obtained his brother's blessing, but something happened in the course of his life that changed his destiny forever. He saw that his life was going nowhere. The tricks and gimmicks that worked for him in his earlier days were not working anymore now that he was a family man. As a matter of fact, they were working against him. Those tricks had come back to haunt him, as his father-in-law Laban had tricked him to work for his daughter Rachel for seven years, and for his own final release of thirteen years. All of those twenty years was so that Jacob could obtain his own freedom to work for his own family, instead of Laban's. He had found out that Laban had no plans of releasing him, but was instead using him to amass wealth. Until Genesis 30, he had nothing that he could call his; for even the food that his family ate was Laban's.

That changed when he made the deal with Laban to keep the speckled and spotted animals from Laban's flock, and God greatly blessed him. This man could have been satisfied after he obtained his freedom from Laban, being a rich man now and no one to answer to, but not so. In Genesis 32, we see that he wrestled with a man (who was God), asking the man to bless him; in other words, change his destiny. His dedication was so intense that the fight lasted until the morning, and the man had to touch the socket of his hip. The socket of Jacob's hip was out of joint as He wrestled with him, but still he refused to let the man go until the man blessed him. It was there that Jacob's name was changed from Jacob (meaning supplanter, or trickster) to Israel (meaning the prince of God). That is what I call passion. He refused to conform to the state of his present success;

thereby, changing his destiny for life. He went for legacy, instead of a few sheep.

PRINCIPLE VS PRESENCE

In today's fast paced world, where almost everyone is out for him/herself, and instant gratification is fast becoming the rule of life, it is becoming more and more challenging to live the "Enoch lifestyle". In this bid for the pleasures of this present world, we have succeeded in gradually pushing God out of our lives, and replaced Him with the principles that He established for planet earth, instead of His presence. A lot of believers are seeking not the presence of the Holy One, but the presence of the influential people of society. They don't seek after the Holy One of Israel for the wisdom to affect their communities, and if there is no seeking after, there will be no manifestation of anything from God. These are the days of larger congregations, but less anointing; more church activities, but less and less praying; large houses, but less time to spend together as a family. We as a church body don't function well, and will have more fun with the people who don't know Christ; therefore, we produce more dysfunctional families than them. We have so much of everything that if we can only stop and take a good look, we will see that we are gradually drowning in the stuff that we have. But much of the stuff we acquire is through our own strength (credit), so it doesn't last.

These are the times the Bible talks about in 1 Timothy 4:1-2, expressly stated by the Amplified Bible (Amp.):

1. *BUT THE [Holy] Spirit distinctly and expressly declares that in latter times some will turn away from the faith, giving attention to deluding and seducing spirits and doctrines that demons teach,*

2. *Through the hypocrisy and pretensions of liars whose consciences are seared (cauterized)."*

As the scripture states above, in these days that we are living in, men will depart from the faith saying, *"these are hard sayings, who can endure them."* They will get rid of enduring for the promises that build the character and faith of the sons of God, and will pay people to lie to them. Basically, they will say, "We know what the Bible says, but we are not willing to endure to the end for the fulfillment of those promises." It will be all about who has the latest car, or largest house, or biggest yacht, or the like. Yes, and we are even seeing that now. These are the days of best-selling authors who use the principles of the Word of God to attract financial prosperity, while denying the validity of the Bible. Men and women are so crazy about knowledge these days that they have turned these overpaid millionaires in to the talk of the 'shows' and 'towns'; sought after by so many for their borrowed insights that their elongated egos have literally made them think that they are above the Word of God. These are the people who church people are flocking after; forgetting where true wealth and prosperity originates from. That is why there is so much carnality, luke-warmness, and materialism in the church of Jesus Christ, because the majority of us believers want to acquire the wealth of this present world by the world's standards.

People who don't necessarily care for the advancement of our Father's Kingdom are dictating our standards to us and because we don't spend time with our Father, we don't know what is right. Because we don't know what is right; everything is right as long as the people whom we allow to think for us put their stamp of approval on it with the churchy seal *'gospel'* or *'Christian.'* This is not the case with the man or woman who is working in the Enoch type of faith, and knows his/her God. They do exploits for God, and are pacesetters, instead of followers.

THE "OLD PATHS"

Like I stated in Chapter 2, there is a path that is necessary to follow if you have lost your way at anytime in this walk with the Lord. These are called the "old paths" that Jeremiah 6:16 talks about. This is not difficult for the saint of God walking the "Enoch lifestyle" in this 21st century. The "old paths" have a history with God, and that history is marked with moments of highs and sometimes lows of sustained battles, where the scars have left a mark or a limp (as with Jacob that wrestled with God), which reminds that saint, and all that look on him/her, that "this one has been with God." So, the "old paths" are good and although God is always doing a new thing, I have found out that He does not abandon the principles of the old paths. They are for the learning of His children. A great deal of that old path is what this chapter is about – getting into the presence of God.

There are many ways that we 'simulate' the presence of God; some people do it by being around other believers, or by listening to Christian material by way of video or audio. All of that is good; however, there are two primary ways of having the presence of God on you all of the time, and hearing for yourself what God is saying for the present time. These two ways are by reading and meditating on the Word of God, and by prayer or communication between you and your God. Watching and listening to Christian materials is really one level, but to go deep in God, we have to adhere to those two ways. His presence is what gives us the victory, and without it we cannot do anything. The Word of God is God's will for us here on earth, and without it we cannot know the benefits that He has for us here. Moreover, without His word, we cannot know how He does things; however, I want to talk about prayer in this section of the "Enoch lifestyle".

My pastor always gives the illustration of him and his wife when talking about this. As he'll say, *"If I say I love my wife, then it should not be grievous to talk to her everyday."* Basically, what the man of God is saying is that if you love someone, you will talk to them everyday, and not maybe once a week. If I talk to my wife for six hours on Sunday, and then for the rest of the week refuse to talk to her because of the conversation that we had on Sunday, I will not be married for long. That is how a lot of us treat God. We will talk to Him on Sunday's, and then go through the whole week without even saying hi to Him. It is impossible to build a relationship with someone who you talk to casually. We, in industrialized nations, sometimes wonder why there is no demonstration of the power of God in our countries, but hear of revivals of poor and far away lands, and wonder why that is not happening in our own lands. Like I stated earlier in this chapter, we have Bibles on i-pods and have every technological edge over some of these countries, but they are doing far more than us in the spiritual realm. It is all because of the passion for the presence of God, and that passion moves them to the place of prayer.

Some of these people don't even have the money to buy a full-sized Bible and still carry the New Testament and Psalms that the last evangelist who visited their villages gave them, but they love God. While we are caught up with the latest shows and or TV program, they can barely boast of electricity to watch their favorite soccer team. So what's left for them is to find out who this God that they have found (or rather has found them) is. Most of the times, instead of learning from them, we criticize them. But what we should be doing is finding out how they keep their hunger for God so alive.

THE SECRET OF REVIVAL

A lot of us call for revival in these last days, but what does it really take to bring that revival? The scriptures charge us to follow, or imitate those who through faith and patience have inherited the promises (Hebrews 6:12). We are to follow their Godly examples of how they inherited the promise; for in doing so, we too will inherit ours. Right now, there is a revival wind sweeping through Africa and most of Asia, and it is very important for us to step on our pride and pick up our notebooks to take notes. It is no secret that Western countries that were taking the Gospel of Jesus Christ to the nations, now need the Gospel to be brought back to them. One thing we have to move away from is past glories. We want to resurrect the Azusa revivals, and bring back the Smith Wigglesworth's and John Wesley's, but at the same time God is waiting to use us, because it is our time, and that time is now. The great men of faith who went before us have done their part. It is now up to us to take the torch and run with it.

What really separates the church in places like Africa, Asia, and any other place where the revival fire is burning, from the church in other parts of the world, is passion. The people have a great appetite for the presence of God, and they don't seem to get enough of Him. Therefore, God shows up big for them. One thing I have noticed about God is that He will not force on you what you don't really want. That can be seen clearly in Exodus 3:4. It was when He noticed that Moses stopped to see what He was doing; basically, He had Moses' full attention; therefore, He told Moses what He was going to do. While we are so consumed with the trivial issues of this present life and buried in the pleasures of our successes, we cannot hear the quiet whisper of the Spirit. They are seeking after the presence of God, and it is evident in the testimonies which are given in their sanctuaries. The dead are raised, blind eyes are open, and the level of spiritual toughness is admirable. You hear of people in Africa walking miles to the place of worship, because they realize that if they can only drag themselves to Zion, their strength will be renewed.

FERVENT EFFECTIVE PRAYER

One of the charges that Jesus left us was to pray without ceasing. That charge amongst many is being very much overlooked today in the church of Jesus Christ. As a matter of fact, it is normal for a lot of believers to go without effectively touching heaven for weeks. This is really one of the main prognoses for the lack of power in the body of Christ today. There is no power that can stand before the child of God that he/she and their God cannot defeat. He has told us that we are more than conquerors, but without Him we cannot do anything. Effective prayer is really an act of obedience, and the "Enoch lifestyle" should not be without it. It really does not take God long to answer prayers. It only takes an obedient heart and a child like faith. When we intercede for cities and nations, bonds are being loosed and territories are taken over from the devil, and the Kingdom of God advances.

In Western churches, we tend to stop praying when we observe just a finger of God (a little result). But intercession should be continuous, and not be for just a moment. The Lord Himself told us in Isaiah 59:16 that He wants an intercessor to stand in the gap. Everyone is familiar with the emergency call for help when we are in distress. In America it is 911. We all know how devastating it can be if emergency personnel don't respond on time. Our prayers are like that in the realm of the spirit if we don't respond to the call of the Spirit to intercede. In this realm that I am talking about when we fail to intercede, evil wins and gains more ground.

That is not so in places like Africa, as well as South Korea, which has the largest congregation in the world. I am talking about the Yoido Full Gospel Church in South Korea. I went there when I was stationed in Korea, and I was amazed at how so many people can be in one place, not for a baseball or a football game, but for Jesus. Even though the auditorium is not as large as some mega-church cathedrals in other parts of the world, the passion for God amongst the people was clearly genuine and captivating. I saw the prayer cubicles where thousands have gone through who have given the place its name- "prayer mountain". People go up there to spend days with God in fasting and prayer for souls to be saved, and also for a closer walk with God. That is why the South Korean Christian population is ever on the rise. There is a willingness to spend time with God for His presence, and not only for material things.

It was not always so in Korea, as it was one of the most resistant nations to the Gospel of Jesus Christ until the latter part of the 20th century, being that it was a deeply Buddhist nation with its shamanistic culture. Many missionaries lost their lives in the initial phase of Christian development in that country. In 1900, the country's Christian population was only about .4 %, but through fervent and effective prayer, by 1992 the Christian population had risen to about 40%. That is what fervent and effective prayer can do. It will loosen the bonds of wickedness and set the captives free, but the people have to be willing to sacrifice their time to pray. The Yoido Full Gospel Church is not the world's largest church because of social gatherings. The people are known for their all night prayer vigils, and early Morning Prayer, which we seldom do in our churches in western churches. I have yet to see, or read of a revival or awakening for God in any part of the world that was not birthed by fervent intensive prayer. There is a price to be paid for that type of result, and it comes through our faith-filled intercessions for the move of God.

Prayer was one of the ingredients in Jesus' ministry that made Him walk so smoothly in the supernatural. He was not short of the supernatural workings of the Spirit, because sometimes, as the Word says, He spent all night in prayer to God. That's why in Gethsemane, where He was betrayed, He asked His disciples, *"Can't you spend an hour with me in prayer."* That makes me know that an hour with Him is at least what we should be shooting for. Yes, you can start with fifteen minutes a day, but you don't have to stay at that level for years.

If you do, it is but certain that you will not grow past fifteen minute types of trials. I'll say it again; an hour is really the minimum we should aim for. If Jesus, the Son of God, spent that much time in prayer, how do we figure we could do it different? He knew that the flesh could not be trusted, so He had to spend a lot of time with His Father for strength, direction, and power.

Africa, which was once known as the "Dark Continent" because of its lack of inventions and also its practice of voodoo, is being taken over by the wings of revival, because of the effectiveness of prayer. I have searched far and wide, and done a little bit of research myself, and I have come to the conclusion that no revival can happen in any part of the world without the people of the land first calling on God for intervention through effective prayer. There should be a yearning for the presence of God, instead of only material things that we lust after. That hunger for God's presence is the one thing we need, and it precedes any revival. Please note that yearning is not for material things, but for the Lord's glory to appear. Sometimes it is a meeting of worship, and sometimes it is just intercession. All of that falling asleep in your prayer is really because you haven't broken out of the flesh and entered the spiritual realm. Most of the time, you can tell whether you broke through in the Spirit or not, because if the prayer has not touched you, how can it touch heaven?

I am not talking of just asking God for something here. What I'm talking about is effectual fervent prayer, which as Pastor Yonggi

Cho of Yoido Full Gospel Assembly church in South Korea (largest congregation in the world for now) states, *"can sometimes last hours"*, and most of the time you are calling to God for someone else, and not for yourself. This is not hours of asking God for the same thing over and over, but just as the prince of Persia withstood Daniel for twenty-one days (Dan 10) until the angel Michael came to his rescue, so the princes over the cities that we live in withstand our prayers. We have to be willing to press through, and that sometimes means hours of the Prayer of Thanksgiving. That passion is what's missing in our churches in western civilizations today, but we will be surprised to see the resolve if we do press, because we have the language of the Holy Spirit, which the devil does not understand.

We are in a better covenant. That is why when you wake up in the middle of the night and you don't know what to do, it is not to go out shopping at Wal-Mart (for those countries that have the inconvenience of 24/7 shopping capabilities). I say inconvenience, because I believe that even a city should learn how to sleep and reflect on God's goodness. It is not even time to turn on the TV and get more bad news about the world's crumbling economy, or to watch your favorite team win or lose a three-hour ball game. These are times that the Holy Spirit wants you to intercede for nations and individuals that are in trouble, and at the edge of the gates of hell. Think of how many lives that could have been spared from hell if believers had spent an extra thirty minutes a day interceding in the Spirit? These are also times that you just sit at the Master's feet and wait in His presence; not that you need something, but because you love Him and want to include Him in your agenda. If we learn to do that, many of our agendas will change, and we will see a mighty outpouring of God's presence in our lives.

KEEPING THE PRESENCE

That was the state Moses was in, in Exodus 33:15 where he told God if His presence didn't go with them (the Israelites), then they might as well not go anywhere. In this realm, the flesh does not get in the way, because the spirit man becomes alive. Moses wanted more of God (basically he could not have enough of Him), so in verse 18 of the same chapter he asked to see the full glory of God. Even though God did not show him all of His glory, He made a place for him (Moses). That place was in the cleft of a rock, which signified Jesus, pointing to what Jesus would do on the cross; reconciling man back to God. That proves the fact that our access to God is only through our Lord and Savior Jesus Christ.

However, you do not get to this realm by praying once a week or having your worship, intercession, and studying of the Word of God all done in ten minutes. There has to be a growth in your relationship with God. Thank God for fasting and the benefits of it, but in this realm your daily life itself becomes a fast unto God. Fasting draws you closer to God, but in this realm you are so close to Him that you have an open heaven always before you. It is so easy to access the throne of God in this realm. It was this realm that a man like Smith Wigglesworth got to in his time that it was said of him, *"he was not given to protracted periods of fasting and prayer"*, but instead, he learned the *secret of being in continuous, intimate communion with God."* This is why he walked in the supernatural so much just like his elder brother Jesus.

The presence of the Lord is what brings the anointing, and the anointing is what breaks the yoke, or makes the difference in any situation. I've found out that this is why some of us proclaim a thing and nothing happens. That is why some ministers of the Gospel can almost bathe the sick with oil and pray, but nothing happens, while others will just speak a word, and the sickness or situation is lifted off or turned around. That type of authority is what God entrusts to His Sons when He knows that He can trust them. If you are still having a struggle to talk to Him (pray) daily and learning His ways by staying in His Word daily, this type of authority will elude you when you need it. To keep His presence, you must love His presence. This was what Job was talking about when he said that the secret of God was with him. If he dared speak, princes will hush and the nobles will not dare challenge his counsel (Job 29). He had gotten to the point of friendship where staying in the presence of his God was no longer burdensome. This is the only way you can keep His presence. There is no other way; this "old path" is fixed, and not interchangeable.

FINDING REST IN HIS PRESENCE

My wife and I went to a restaurant one day, and when she got out of the vehicle, I noticed that she was standing at the door waiting for me. I knew what it was about, so I intentionally delayed my exit from the vehicle. After a while, I came out and opened the door for her. We passed the first double doors, but there was another set in front of us, and she again stood there waiting for me to open the door. I then got heated, and said something to her in my local dialect that translated into, *"I'm tired woman."* Immediately, I said that I knew what I had done and what was coming my way. She opened her own door, as I had blown away the opportunity. If you are married, you understand how I was feeling at that time. She then asked me if I was too tired to open the door for her (which I do all the time), but had no problem opening it for other women whose names I don't even know. I went on to justify myself by saying, "Well, don't expect it as a rule, instead of me doing it out of love." She didn't say much after that. She didn't have to. I won the argument on that day, but my day of reckoning was coming, and it came about two weeks after that incident when I opened the door for two women who were walking into the military dining facility. I was so enthused to open the door for them, but surprisingly the reaction I got from them was rather cold. They may have said "Thank you", but I don't remember hearing it. The Holy Spirit then brought the incident with my wife to mind, and I was convicted and asked for mercy.

Someone may ask, "Is it a sin not to open the door for your wife?" Of course not, but I can say doing for others what you can't willingly do for your spouse, does send a mixed message. Opening the door for my wife requires not much physical energy on my part, and as a matter of fact, I do it all the time. However, at that time I was really spiritually drained, having ministered to a lot of people God's Word. What I was not doing was refilling my spiritual tank. Because of work and other obligations, I would spend a few minutes in prayer and the Word, and then speed off to work. At work, people would come to me with life issues, and I would pour into their lives with the little that I had left in my tank. After a while, I was empty and running on fumes, so what was usually easy to do, became burdensome. We have seen and heard of believers who are supposed to be Christ-like, who act so carnal in public that we question whether they are saved or not. We have heard of ministers of the Gospel having fights both with spouses, and with other members of the Body of Christ.

Why is the divorce rate so high amongst the people who are supposed to reconcile the world to God? Why do we hear of ministers of the Gospel (music included) having breakdowns in their families and elsewhere to the point that they want to quit doing what God has called them to do? Why do we produce dysfunctional families, just like the world we are trying to win over? Why is it that anytime there is a misunderstanding which does not seem to be resolved between young spouses, they want to head straight to the divorce court? These are very serious questions, but they are very answerable, and the answer is so close to us, if we look in the right place – the Word of God. The number one answer to a lot of these questions is that we are fatigued and burnt out, just as I was at that restaurant with my wife. When a man is burnt out; if he tries to do any work it will not be to the best of his ability. We have to realize that our strength comes from the Lord, and from no other source. Psalm 16:11 tells us that there is fullness of joy in God's presence:

"You will show me the path of life; In Your presence is fullness of joy; At Your right hand are pleasures forevermore."

What we have done is put the cart before the horse in this race. We love the pleasures that He gives, but really don't love to be in His presence. How can't we be fatigued, when we keep on going and going, and fail to recharge our batteries? Even common sense tells us that when a container is almost depleted of its contents, if we want to continue to pour the same contents of that container, we have to refill it.

Ministers of the Gospel (including music) will have their schedules booked out for the rest of the year, but will not schedule a day for the One they are going to sing or talk about. As a matter of fact, some ministers will not honor a call to minister if there is no honorary (the money given to ministers after ministration). Some are just satisfied with inviting each other to preach in each other's churches, and receive five-digit figure sums, but care nothing about the

Word that will change lives – the Word of God. This makes many think if it is all about Him, or about the Benjamin's (money). We have lost His presence, but if we have our priorities right (that is put Him first in the schedule), we will find out that we will have the strength to minister effectively. We need to take a break and get into the presence of the Lord, so that times of refreshing will come from the presence of the Lord. That is why we get so edgy and snap like a twig when we are bent a little by light afflictions; that is why our divorce rate is just as high as the people we are suppose to win over. We have to love on Him (our Lord) again, as we did when we first got saved. Sometimes, we (I don't mean only fulltime ministers) need to cancel everything on our agenda, and just wait in His presence to hear from Him

BALANCE

In closing, I'd love to emphasize the word balance as it relates to the saint of God. I believe that balance is the key in living the Enoch type of life. It is imperative that we be balanced in our walk with God. When I was a young believer, I quit my job to spend time with God fulltime. I almost starved to death. I was not a minister operating in the five-fold ministry; I just had zeal for God. That was immaturity on my part, and it had to take me countless number of days, without adequate diet in Africa, to realize that God wants us to do His whole Word. When He said if a man does not work, let Him not eat in 2 Thessalonians 3:10, He wasn't suggesting it, but really meant it. The pangs of hunger taught me that. Likewise, in the Church today, we are sometimes neglecting key tenets of the Word that really make us incomplete. A good example is the idea that we can evangelize better when we become wealthy, so we ignore sharing our faith and focus on our vision to prosper financially.

You see, when we focus on the riches and ignore the lost that we encounter on a daily basis; then I believe we have an imbalance issue. I believe in prosperity and the fact that the wealth of the nations will be converted to the saints, but when we start to forget the basics, such as winning the lost and becoming everything to all men so that we can win them to Christ, we become imbalanced. On the other hand, there are a lot of believers who operate very big in the gifts of the Spirit, who pray for the sick and they recover in minutes, but cannot boast of a good savings account, or an investment portfolio. Some of us don't even believe in investing financially, thinking that these are earthly riches which will pass away; therefore, we do not need to acquire it. At the same time, we see the people who don't know our God prospering more and more, while we are getting poorer and poorer.

Money loves to reproduce, but if we don't respect it, it will form wings and fly somewhere else where it is respected. That is why in the parable of the talents in Matthew 25:14-30, the servant who was unproductive was stripped of what he had, and his talent was given to the one who had the most. I used to wonder why the Lord did not give the talent to the other guy who had two, but instead to the one who had the most money. Not anymore, because now I realize that money is attracted to much more money. A lot of us know it by this phrase, "The rich keep getting richer and the poor keep getting poorer."

God has given us the blueprint of success (His Word), and it is now up to us to dominate in all areas of our lives. Why is it that a lot of us can quote every other scripture about healing, deliverance, and the rest, but cannot locate up to three scriptures that talk about money? That is because a lot of us want to remain poor and humble as Jesus, so that we can be as holy as He is. But who said Jesus was poor, and why do we think poverty is synonymous with humility or holiness? If we check the scriptures we'll find out that Jesus talked about money more than any other subject, except His Father's Kingdom. In His ministry, the man was so wealthy that He had a treasurer – Judas, who betrayed Him. When He was born, God mobilized a whole group of wise men from across the world to show up at His parent's house to bless Him with gifts that could solve anyone's financial problems for the rest of their earthly lives. I know that there is a lot of debate amongst theologians about the value of the gifts, but the fact remains that gifts were brought for the child Jesus, and His parents received them. I don't know about you, but if I am going that far to worship who I believe is the King of all kings, and the Messiah of the world, I would make sure to I bring the best I have, and I believe that is what the wise men did.

Even with all that wealth (both earthly and heavenly), Jesus was well balanced in His life. He never lived exorbitantly, but always associated with the poor and the people WHO were looked down at in society. The furtherance of His Father's Kingdom was paramount in His mind. At one time he was heard saying, *"Foxes have holes and birds of the air have nests, but the Son of Man has nowhere to lay His head"* (Luke 9:58). Does this mean that the Lord had no money to buy a house? Of course not, because Mark 2:15 tells us that He broke bread in His own house. What this means is that He was too busy to stay in one place, as He travelled so much. We should learn from that and be balanced in our own walk in Christ. Today, a lot of believers tend to flock to congregations that preach prosperity with no personal responsibility on the saint for the presence of God. In this type of teaching, there is no chasing after God, but there is no shortage for the chasing after the prosperity of God. It is a dangerous type of mentality that will allow the believer to fall into the snare of the seed in the parable of the sower (Mark 4:16-17). When we don't chase after God, but chase prosperity, we leave ourselves open to the trap of the evil one.

This thing called balance is critical in your walk with the Lord. With passion, you can acquire the secret of God, but with balance you can communicate that secret to your world. There are a lot of areas in our walk with Christ that we need balance in. Take for example the area of power over sicknesses and diseases. A lot of believers have all that money could afford, but are losing loved ones to terminal diseases, or are themselves dying of one. Some pastors in the Kingdom don't even pray for the sick any more. They don't even try and see if God will heal out of His compassion. Their first choice is the physical doctor who is limited in his/her ability, but our King took thirty-nine stripes for us on Calvary, and that covers all diseases, because all major diseases are divided into thirty-nine different categories. I thank God I am not in such a congregation.

In this 21st century, where everything is becoming miniaturized through the science of microchip technology, that we can carry the Word of God now in devices as small as our cell phones, you'll think that some schools of thought don't exist anymore in the church. But you'll be surprised to find out that a lot of us still think that sicknesses and diseases are God's will to teach us a lesson. The Lord has given us dominion over them, but if we do not exercise our right, we will lose that battle every time to sicknesses and diseases. I personally believe that a lot of us die too early. It is not God's will for us to populate Heaven, while we have a mission not accomplished here on earth. He will not reject His saints when they die, because Psalm 116:15 states:

"Precious in the sight of the Lord is the death of His saints,"

But He wants us to finish our mission here on earth strong, and not be taken out by illnesses. He is in Heaven cheering us on with the cloud of witnesses (Hebrews 12:1). There is an imbalance in our diet that we receive across the pulpit. It is that we only consume what we think is good for us, just as a child will eat the meat in his/her dinner, and leave the vegetables for the trash. Ministers, we should remember that the pulpit is meant to pull us out of the pit, but if we don't preach the full counsel of God, we rob the people of God from the full benefits of salvation.

By the grace of God, and by choice, I have believed God for divine health for more than thirteen years, and He has not failed me yet. I have had many opportunities to go to the doctor, but I am yet to use that option, because God always shows up for me; healing me before my faith fails me. I am not suggesting that going to the doctor or even taking medication is lack of faith, but this one thing I know, (I personally) have developed my faith to a complete dependence on divine healing and health that I have no reason to believe otherwise, and you can too. God never intended for us to develop one part of our faith, and leave the rest un-attended, like a weight lifter who focuses only on his/her upper body, and forgets the lower part of the body. The result will be a very imbalanced church, which is not ready for its King. But we will be ready, because His Holy Spirit is preparing the Church through anointed men and women of God teaching and preaching His Word, and through anointed books like, "The Enoch Lifestyle."

That brings me to another critical and sensitive area in our daily lives. It is the area of taking care of our temples. I am not only talking about abstinence from sin, but also of learning to live right physically. Our bodies are the temple of God. God has given us the responsibility of taking care of them. This body that He has given to us is supposed to last us the length of time that He has us here to carry out

His purpose and plan for our lives, whether it is seventy or one-hundred years in good health and strength, because it was built tough to last us that duration. However, if we don't take care of it, having bad eating habits and refusing to exercise, it won't last half of that time. When it comes to the area of exercise, a lot of us have the mentality that since the scriptures state that bodily exercises profits little (1 Tim 4:8), exercise is not necessary for the believer.

We believe that we are exempt because we are doing the work of the Lord; therefore, He will not allow our bad decisions, as it relates to our eating and exercise, to affect our health. But that mentality is wrong, especially as technology is gradually helping us take the physical part of work out of our daily routines. Some of us have the latest dress shoes and suits, but can't even boast of a shoe for our favorite sports that we love to workout in. We have to change that for us to live longer and accomplish God's plan for our lives. One thing I have noticed about God is that He will not do for us the thing which He has given us the ability to do in the natural. We see it everyday – good and godly people taken out of this world before their time by illnesses that could have been prevented. That is why He says His people are destroyed for lack of Knowledge (Hosea 4:6). As I said earlier, that will change. The Lord is preparing His church, and He will not rest until His church, Zion, becomes praise in the earth. That is why He is moving His people to get into their purpose, so that His Kingdom will be established here on earth, as it is in Heaven. This is the reason for "The Enoch Lifestyle".

References & Notes

Chapter One:

1. Dennis Sempebwa. Quote from Leadership Conference. pp 20.

2. Albert Einstein. Quote from well-known Physicist. pp 21.

Chapter Two:

3. Seung-Hui Cho. Confession of Virginia Tech Shooter. pp 25.

Chapter Three:

4. Lance Armstrong. Seven consecutive Tour de France victories. pp 52.

5. Calvin Coolidge. Quote from Former President. pp 52.

6. Dr. W.J. Moreland. LIVE (Living In Victory Everyday). pp 55.

7. Napoleon Hill. Quote from Think and Grow Rich. pp 58.

Chapter Four:

8. Dr. W.J. Moreland. Quote. pp 68.

9. Cooper Tires. Company Slogan. pp 71.

Bibliography

Armstrong, L. (July 24, 2005) 2005 Tour De France. [Online].
Available: http://en.wikipedia.org/wiki/2005_Tour_de_France

Ashimolowo, M. KICC (King's Way International Christian
Centre) TV. [Online]. Available:
http://www.kicc.org.uk/Home/tabid/36/Default.aspx

Cho, Seung-Hui. (April 16, 2007) Virginia Tech Shooter
Manifesto Rant. [Online]. Available:
http://www.youtube.com/watch?v=Vyal Pi1GeDY

Coolidge, C. Quote World-(John) Calvin Coolidge. [Online].
Available: http://www.quoteworld.org/quotes/3186

Cooper tires quote – "Don't Give Up a Thing." [Online]. Available:
http://www.treadepot.com/tires/coop.html

Daniels, P.J. (2003). Peter J. Daniels A Brief History. [Online]
Available: https://www.danel.ch/study_authors_original.html and
Living on the Edge: (Autobiography) (World Centre for
Entrepreneurial Studies, 2003)

Einstein, A. Albert Einstein Quotes. [Online]. Available:
http://www.brainyquote.com/quotes/authors/a/alberteinstein.html

Hill, N. (2005). Think and Grow Rich.   Filiquarian Publishing,
LLC.

Monroe, M. (2003). Rediscovering the Kingdom. Shippensburg,
PA: Destiny Image Publishers.

Moreland, Dr. W.J. LIVE – (Live In Victory Everyday) – International Gospel Church, Kitzingen, Germany. [Online]. Available: www.igcgermany.org

Moreland, Dr. W.J. Quote: "God is the only One that will bless you to the point that you forget Him." [Online]. Available: http://igcgermany.org

Robison, J. James and Betty Robison. [Online] Available: http://www.lifetoday.org/site/PageServer?pagename=abt_robison

Schultz, H. (June 4, 1987). "Starbucks Coffee Is Sold To Owner Of Il Giornale" <u>Seattle Post- Intelligencer.</u> 4 June 1987: pp B8. [Online]. Available: http://www.seattlepi.com/archives/1987/8701140879.asp

Sempebwa, Dennis. International Gospel Church Germany, August 2008; Leadership Conference. Founder and President of Eagle's Wings International, a global leadership development organization.

WW II. How Many People Died in World War II? [Online] Available: http://wiki.answers.com/Q/How_many_people_died_in_World_War_2

Please visit www.hunterheartpublishing.com to purchase other book by this author.

Inspirations from Downrange

Book can also be purchased alongside:

What Will People Say?

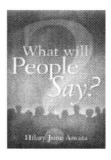

www.aandhamara.com

Also available online at www.amazon.com and www.barnesandnoble.com

Hunter Heart Publishing

"Offering God's Heart to a Dying World"
www.hunterheartpublishing.com

Other books by
Hunter Heart
Publishing

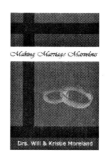

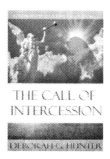